Absolution

Prologue

My name is Toby Robyns and I live in West Sussex. I'm married with three big kids, Zoe 27, Zach 24 and Victoria 22 from my first marriage and two little ones, Baxter 10 and Brody 9 from my second marriage. My wonderful wife of 13 years is Heidi. She works as a receptionist at a GP surgery in Portslade. I work as Emergency Care Assistant on the ambulance. It's a fantastic job and I love it, but as you can imagine, sometimes it's very stressful. Every year, around January we book a holiday to somewhere with a bit of sunshine, somewhere where we can recharge our batteries for a fortnight. I'm not well paid so we pay off the holiday in instalments over six months or so. What I am trying to get across, is simply that we are a normal family with normal jobs, normal kids and normal lifestyles. We struggle just like everybody else.

We travelled to Turkey back in 2011 and always wanted to go back. However, with the state of play in Turkey, we decided to avoid the country and holiday in safer places in and around the Mediterranean. In January 2017 we checked the Government website and it stated that it was safe to travel to Turkey so long as you kept away from the Syrian border. Happy days, we booked our all-inclusive holiday in Turgutreis just outside Bodrum, saving ourselves around £1000 against the same holiday in Spain or Greece.

On 4th August 2017, me, Heidi and the boys departed Gatwick for our well-earned break in the Turkish sunshine. No major problems with the hotel or the holiday to be fair. We booked a a boat trip through the hotel, to depart from Turgutreis harbour, the boys chose the boat which was made to look like a pirate galleon. It even had a relief of Pirates of the Caribbean, Davy Jones on the back of the boat. I suppose the boat carried about forty or fifty holiday makers, all looking for some fun in the sun. The boat dropped anchor at four or five different places throughout the day and provided us with lunch too.

On arrival at a place called the Wishing Cave, the captain informed us that there were some algae growing around the mouth of the cave and to be careful with the boys. Apparently, these particular algae would bring you up in an itchy rash. Executive decision by Heidi was made. We decided to go snorkelling instead. The captain became excited and said that we should join him, and he would show us some big fish instead, just being a good host I guess. Heidi stayed on the boat in the sun and me and the boys grabbed our masks and snorkels.

On leaving the boat the captain grabbed a handful of what looked like coins from a pot by the wheel. We were joined by five or six other tourists, with the same idea and in we went. We all followed the captain about 100 m towards the shore where as promised he showed us large schools of brightly coloured fish. Being the good host that he was he encouraged the boys to dive down and touch the bottom. He added an incentive by placing a coin on the bottom for the boys to recover at a depth of only about two meters or so. The boys swam down and retrieved a couple of coins each as did the other tourists that had joined us. He put my coin down a lot deeper as a bit of a challenge I suppose, but I played the game and went down and collected the coin.

After thirty minutes or so, we all got out of the water and back on to the boat. I asked the captain what the coins were, they looked old, to which he replied that they were ''pirate treasure''. ''Pirate boat, pirate treasure''. He raised the anchor and off we went to the next destination. The boys were excited about their treasure and managed to tap the captain up for a few more.

During the remainder of the holiday the boys played with the coins in the hotel pool, diving down and retrieving them from the bottom. Towards the end of the holiday, I asked the hotel receptionist about the coins. She explained that they were just souvenirs and that the captain used them to create the pirate image with the children. They had no monetary value and they were just souvenirs from the pirate boat

Me being me, honest as the day is long, I decided to put them in a transparent customs bag and declare them at the airport, just in case. The story that follows is my account of what happened when I did just that. I have dictated the story into my phone over a period of six hours or so and then the lovely Amanda at Bright VA has transcribed it into Word; these are my words and have not been influenced by anybody else. The account has come from a diary of bullet points which I managed to smuggle out of prison in my boxer shorts!!

* * *

Chapter One

I got myself a plastic tray, put my green man-bag in it and the coins in a clear customs bag, the one you use for fluids and things like that when you declare them, going through customs. I put everything in the tray and through the X-ray machine it went. I wandered through x-ray, all clear, however my bag had raised alarm with one of the security officers. I was asked to wait at the end of reclaim by the security officer. She looked at me and said, "stones". I didn't get what she meant at first, I had no idea what she was talking about. Anyway, she said "stones" again and I was still flummoxed. So, then she looked at my neck and pointed and said "stones" and I sort of, "Oh yeah, okay, stones, I get it". I wear a little stone round my neck for luck. We opened the bag up, emptied the contents out – there was a few: phone chargers and bits and pieces; not much in there at all really – popped it all in the plastic tray and then she picked out a few stones, which were small marble chunks that the boys had found on the beach; they wanted to make an aquarium when we came home. She said, "You can't take these through customs, you can't take these on the plane," so we emptied them all out, put them into a bin and that, I thought, was the end of it.

However, when we started putting everything back in the bag, she picked up my little plastic bag with the coins in and got all excited. I said, "Am I allowed to take these through? If I'm not, please just take them." She asked me to wait, so I put my bag back together and waited at the end of the conveyor belt, with Heidi and the boys. Anyway, she went off to the manager's office and, I don't know, a few minutes later she came back and said, "You need to come with me and see the manager, it's procedure." So, off I went.

There was this huge, overweight, sweating, bald man, who was obviously the manager, with my coins and my passport sitting on his table. I said to him, "How can I help you?" and he looked at me and said, "No English", so I thought well, this is going to go well. He said, "Just wait, procedure," that's all he said. So, I waited and waited. Eventually I walked to the office doorway and just checked on the boys and Heidi. I said, "Are you guys okay?" I said, "I'm waiting for something, I don't know what, procedure, apparently." Anyway, about five minutes later this chap came in, got his phone out and took some pictures of the coins and then he disappeared. I said to the manager, "What do you want me to do? Can I go?" "No, no, you stay, stay, wait, procedure." He said. So, okay, I'm hanging around, hanging around and, I don't know, maybe another five minutes pass and somebody else comes in and the first thing I said to him was, "Do you speak English?" and he says, "Small English, small English". So, I said, "What's going on?" He said, "You can't take coins." I said, "Well, okay, fine. Is there a fine or what do I need to do?" And he said, "No, no, no. You wait, it's just procedure." So I just kept waiting and waiting. With that, yet another guy came in, a younger lad, and he said, "I speak English". So I said ''okay''. He said, "These coins, they might be valuable. We might need to go to the police station and sort it all out, procedure." So okay, fair enough I guess.

Then, another guy enters the office and he identifies himself as plain clothes police and with that, he takes his gun out and gets his handcuffs out. At which point I react quite strongly and said, "Look, there is no way on God's green earth you're taking me out of here in handcuffs at gunpoint in front of my children." He's waving his gun in my face and everything else, so I talked to the lad that could speak English and I said, "Look, there's no need for guns and handcuffs. I'm quite happy to come to the police station and sort this misunderstanding out and we'll go from there." He said, "Okay, fine." He explained to the policeman that if he put his handcuffs and his gun away I'd come quietly, and we could go and sort out the misunderstanding. I said first I need to tell my wife what's going on and he said, "Okay, fair enough". I walked out, said to Heidi and the boys, "Look, go to the aeroplane, go to the departure gate and I'll meet you there, I've got go around the corner with these guys, procedure." They were reluctant to say the very least but after some persuasion they agreed. The boys were tired, and Baxter was in tears, it was really late. I didn't even say goodbye, I just said I'll see you in a while, but I had a feeling that I wasn't going to be on the plane tonight. If Heidi had known that I was going to the police station she would have created merry hell! I hated lying to her, not my style at all.

We get out of the airport, into a police car, and the police decide to put its blue lights on for what was probably about a thirty-five second journey to the police station, which is on the airport site, all a bit ridiculous and unnecessary. We walked into the police station, I'm ushered into this office where there's, I don't know, two or three policemen, all plain clothes, all with guns on their hips and all smoking. Nobody spoke any English and it was just so frustrating because I'd tried to explain what I'd done, what I'd thought I'd done and how this could be resolved.

I was asking lots of questions. They just looked at me as though I was an alien, really. They told me to sit down on this old . . . it was like an old bus seat, an old bus bench in the office, so I sat down on there and they were chatting away amongst themselves. They had the coins and they kept looking at me and looking at the coins. I said, "Does anybody speak English? Anybody speak English?" and nothing. Finally, they put some paperwork under my nose. They had photocopied my passport, and the papers were thankfully in English: Would you like to sign here to say that this is a true likeness of yourself. As it was in English, I thought, well, it's only a likeness, I'll sign, so I signed. Then they printed a load more paperwork out, all written in Turkish, and they're saying, "Sign here, sign here, sign here, procedure," to which I replied, "No, no, no, no, no. I'm not signing anything, not until I've spoken to the British consul". As soon as mentioned British Consul it all went quiet. They became very thoughtful just staring at me like I had dropped a bomb. This continued for a few minutes and the silence was broken by the entrance of a short round man, a Thomas Cook rep, dressed in his fluorescent jacket – he spoke English. I said, "Look, what's going on? Am I here for the night or what's going on?" He said, "Yeah, you're gonna be here tonight, but if everything goes well you can go home tomorrow." Okay, fair enough, I think. So I decide that it's a good idea to co-operate, however I still want to speak to the consul first. I'm telling the Thomas Cook rep this and I said, "Look, I've still got the boarding passes and the passports for the boys and Heidi and I need to give these to them. Can you sort this out for me?" He was, "Yep, I can do all that for you." So I emptied my wallet – I had some Turkish lira and twenty pounds. I knew that Heids was going to have to get the taxi from Gatwick back to the house, and I also gave him the front door keys because I was the only one with front door keys. I gave all this to the Thomas Cook rep and basically said, "Before you go, tell them that I'm not saying anything until I've spoken to the British consul and I'm not saying anything until Heidi and the boys are on the plane." So, that was that.

Off he went so I continued to sit on the bus bench in the office – then, I don't know, maybe half an hour later he came back and started chatting away with the police. He then turned to me and said, "Look, what they're going to do, is get some people coming from Bodrum Museum to come and have a look at the coins, just to see what they are, how valuable they are, and what they want to do about it." So, I thought well, this is a step forwards, I guess. Anyway, with that, they ushered me out into another office where there was a guy standing there with a telephone in his hand, he said, "It's the British consul". I remember speaking to a guy called Stefan, who was a really nice chap, and he helped me out by explaining what to do and what not to do. Don't sign anything in Turkish, just sign papers that are in English and just co-operate as much as possible as this was a simple mistake that should be easily sorted out. He said what would happen if I was charged, that they would take me to court on the Saturday, the following day, and then he would call back after the hearing on my mobile to advise me further. Okay, fine. He promised to ring me back the following morning and we'd talk about any developments. As soon as I hand the phone back, I get escorted back into the first office, where a couple of police pick up some car keys and said, "Right, we're going to the hospital. You need to have a medical". At this time, I've still got my phone, I've still got everything. I'm texting Heidi, saying I need to do this, I need to do that, don't worry about me, just get on the plane.

After a short drive, about 10 minutes, we arrive at the hospital, I'm escorted inside through what looks like a very basic A & E. We're ushered through. There are lots of people waiting but jump all the queues and am whisked through, pushed past everybody and put into a triage cubicle, where I wait for only a few seconds, really, less than a minute. The doctor comes in – he looks at me and he says, "Have you any hurt?" I looked at him thinking what are you talking about? I said, "No, I don't hurt anywhere, I'm good." He signed it and waved us away. There endeth the medical, so we got back in the car. I sat in the back of the car thinking have I just had a medical? I couldn't believe it, comparing it with the UK in my head.

Off we went back to the police station. When we got back there, there were four people – two men and two women – from Bodrum Museum and they were looking at the coins. The first thing they did was shake hands with me and say thank you. I thought, blimey! Have I done someone a favour?! One of the ladies had good English and she said, "You've done this country a great service". I said, "Oh really?" She said, "How did you find them?" I said, "Well, I was snorkelling – the boys found them, the captain put them there . . ." I basically explained what I'd already told everybody so far. They got very excited and decided to take the coins. Off they went with the coins and everybody seemed to disappear at that time. The guy from Thomas Cook came back and said, "Your wife and children and are on the plane". He showed me a photograph of them boarding the plane. He told me he had given them the money, the passports, the boarding cards, the front door keys, and it was all good.

The remaining policeman said, "You need to sign some of this paperwork so that we can keep you here tonight". I looked at the paperwork – it was all in Turkish. I said, "I'm not signing anything unless it's in English". He put a bit of a face on and got the one bit of paper that I had signed and then proceeded to forge my signature on every document he had in front of him. When he had finished signing my name he gestured for me to follow him, where I was shown into a cell. There was a room with a huge iron door on it. I walked in and he said something in Turkish which I presume meant good night. He then locked the door and disappeared.

That was that, no bedtime story. I stood there taking in my surroundings, probably in some degree of shock. Off the room were two cells, both with the doors open, and a bathroom. I had a quick wander round and just stood there in total disbelief. Eventually I wandered into the bathroom. The toilet was just unbelievable. What was white was now completely brown and just disgusting. The shower wasn't much better and there was a sink, where the last thing you'd want to wash in there was your hands let alone your face. I walked into the cells and laid on the bed – I say bed, it was like a mattress on some concrete blocks. I thought maybe the other one's more comfortable, so I went into the other cell and messed about for about ten minutes, eventually deciding on the first cell. I stripped off my T-shirt and shorts and just lay on the bed, just in complete disbelief as to what had happened and why it had happened. The fact that I'd been so honest and declared the coins had made no difference at all. I was worried out the kids, I was worried about Heidi, I was just completely shocked, and frustrated more than anything. I couldn't really believe what was going on and why on earth this had it happened to me? After about half an hour/an hour, I must have nodded off. I had no watch – that had all been taken. My necklace had gone with the stone on, my wedding ring had been taken. I had nothing, basically. I had no idea what time it was – there was no clock on the wall.

When I woke up it was daylight. I presumed it was early, but I didn't know. I banged on the door and a policeman came. He looked at me as though to say what do you want. I said, "I want to come out, I don't want to be in here – there's no need for me to be in here. I've not been charged with anything at all. I need a drink of water – I have no water." He said, "Okay, wait." About half an hour later he came back and walked me into what I presumed was the police mess room. There was a table tennis table in there, policemen all in uniform and a very important looking policeman in full dress uniform with epaulettes, medals etc. He gave me a bottle of water and asked if I'd like some breakfast. I just thought anything to get out of the cell – yes, I'll have some breakfast. He then took me back to the cell and another half an hour later, I presume, he came and got me and I went back into the same office that I'd been in the night before where I sat at somebody's desk with a breakfast from an aeroplane – airline food. I sat there – I wasn't really hungry at all, but he gave me a cup of Turkish tea (Chai) where I sat and prolonged the breakfast as long as I could, anything to stay out of that cell. He said, "We need to make you a statement." This is all in pigeon English. He asked me what I did for a living. I explained I'm ambulance crew. He asked me things like my date of birth and general stuff. He said, "How did you find the coins?" I told him the story. He managed to write four lines which he translated on Google translate. I was slightly worried about the length of my statement. However, he was happy with it! He wanted to put me back in the cell. I said, "I don't need to go back in the cell, I'll wait here." He said, "No, no, no. Cell, cell, cell – you have to go back to the cell." I said, "What am I supposed to do in there?" He said, "You sleep. Everyone sleeps in the cell." Okay. So I reluctantly went back to the cell for three or four hours, I'm guessing.

The door finally opens, and I'm taken out of the cell, I'm put back into the same office, where there's a young lad sitting there. He's probably eighteen/twenty. He introduced himself as Mohamed. I said, "Hello, Mohamed. How are you?" He said, "I'm your translator." I'm thinking well, this is a start in the right direction. I start striking up a conversation with Mohamed and it transpires that his English is extremely poor. To make yourself understood was really, quite difficult. Now I'm getting a little bit worried, thinking if this guy's my translator, what chance have I got? He explains to me you have to go to court. Well, hopefully, we'll go to court, we'll get this all sorted out and then I can jump on a plane and get back to my little world with my family, driving an ambulance. We chat for a little bit longer, then the policeman says we need to get in the police car, we need to go to court.

So, we drive around to the other side of the airport where we pick up another chap, whose got a big pile of paperwork, which I notice has got my signature all over it, none of which I've signed. He sits in the front, I'm in the back with the translator and off we go. The guy in the front turns to me and he said, "Why didn't you pay the fine?" I said, "What are you talking about?" He said, "You could have bribed us last night 500 TL." I said, "Well, I don't know anything about bribing policemen. In England it's a crime." He just laughed. Off we went and I'm thinking at least we're going to go to court now, where we can get this mess sorted out. Guess where we go? Back to the hospital. You have to go to the hospital to have another medical to make sure you're fit to stand trial.

We go in – it's exactly the same procedure. A different doctor, but guess what? Exactly the same. "Have you any hurt" "No, I've got no hurt." Off we go. We get to court – bearing in mind this is a Saturday afternoon now – there's nobody there. We jump back in the police car, we go to Bodrum Museum, where we pick up some more paperwork to describe the coins, how old they are, etc. It's all beyond me – I didn't know what they were anyway. We get back in the car again. We drive round to a different museum. Apparently, the first museum we went to had only been given half of the story. They pick up some more paperwork and off we go back to the court.

We hang around at the court for about an hour. It's explained to me that a lawyer will be provided – I'd already asked for a lawyer the night before – and she will be representing me. In the first instance, I go to a very small court – it's basically a small office – where I meet what they call the district attorney. I'd seen this district attorney woman walk into the court with her kids, dressed as though she had just come off the beach. She's not happy that she's been pulled off the beach to come to court. Basically, if she can deal with it in this office there and then, then she will and I will be released. If she can't, then we need to go upstairs to be heard in the higher court, procedure, that bloody word again. I get asked questions – very, very brief questions that my translator translates for me so that she could understand, but it was just a mess. He couldn't translate what I was saying, she didn't understand what he was saying, and my lawyer didn't open her mouth once. Then my translator after about five minutes turns around to me and says we've got to go upstairs, we've got to go to court. I saw that one coming. Okay, fair enough.

As we get outside the office, I looked at my lawyer and I said, "By the way, my name's Toby Robyns," and she doesn't speak any English! She's basically not understood a word I've said, and she just smiles at me as though thinking I don't know what he's saying, but you seem like a nice chap! Mohamed explains she's a new lawyer, she passed the bar two months ago. Oh, my good God! What chance have I got here? We go upstairs and hang around for a while. We wait outside the court when finally, I'm ushered inside.

This court room actually looks like a court where there's a judge, a dock etc. There's me thinking that the chap taking the notes is the judge and the younger lady, who looks all of about twelve, is the lady taking the notes, but it transpires it's completely the opposite, it's the other way around! I'm standing in court, I'm frustrated more than anything, I tell my story yet again. I know it's going wrong, because they ask me how many children I've got and I said I've got three big ones and two little ones, and I know for a fact that my translator is saying something completely different, because I know "besh" means two in Turkish and he told them that I'd got two children instead of five. There were lots of little discrepancies that I couldn't really get my head round. I explained, I was amicable and that I had done everything to cooperate with the authorities. Then this young lady judge turns around to my translator and says, "We're going to remand him to Mugla Maximum Security Prison for smuggling the coins". When he translates for me, I can't believe what I'm hearing. I still believe this is just a ridiculous misunderstanding. It's just complete disbelief. At no time had I tried to smuggle, conceal or hide the coins. If I'd wanted to smuggle I would have put the coins in my wallet or in my suitcase.

From there we walk outside. I get on the phone to Heidi straight away and say I've been remanded to prison. It's been explained to me that I can appeal within a week. I instruct my my lawyer, through my translator, that that's what I want to do, I want to appeal the decision because I completely disagree with it. I said to Heidi that they believe I'm a smuggler and that I was trying to smuggle coins. Even though I declared them at Customs, they still believe I'm smuggling. Heidi's really upset, obviously. I said I'd try and ring her later. We get in the car and guess where we go again? Back to the hospital. Off we go to the same hospital, where I go in, I get "have you any hurt?"

We set off to a different police station now. On arrival, we hang around for a while, waiting for the photographer. When this guy finally decides to make an appearance, I go inside and get my photos taken from the front, left and right sides. Just like on the telly when you see a prisoner holding a board with name date of birth etc. How did I ever end up here? Next, it's over to the finger print machine. Finger prints done we leave the police station, still no idea where the hell I am though. My translator then decides to add insult to injury by telling me that he's not a qualified translator at all. He works in the ''Duty Free shop''!! You couldn't make it up!!!

I get back in the car and off we go back to the police station at Milas Airport where I'm told I've got to wait outside. At that point, there's me thinking there's nobody here, I'm sitting on a bench outside, there's no policemen around – all I'd have to do is walk into the airport and I'd be done. In hindsight, I wish I'd done it, but I'm not that brave.

The police then came out – two different policemen who I didn't know, never seen before. They said to get in the back of the car, so I got in the back. They didn't speak to me at all for the entire journey. They basically drove me for about two hours to Mugla. They smoked all the way and stopped at different places for tea. It was so un-British-police-like! A bit of an eye-opener, to say the least. We pulled up at the prison.

It was dark – all I could think of was Colditz. I didn't know what to expect. I had visions of Ronnie Barker and Porridge! I thought it would be me and some Turkish lad sharing bunk beds in a cell, that's what I envisaged prison would be like. As we pulled up to this place the first thing I saw was a tank, lots of military vehicles, a helicopter, lots of soldiers. We got out of the car and walked in through the gates. There was a guard in a little sentry box who opened the gate. We walked past and he told us where to go. There were some prisoners – I believe they were prisoners, they looked like prisoners – hanging around in the yard. It was a big open space and there were a few pub-style benches with people sitting on them. I presumed them to be prisoners, but I don't know who they were, really.

We went through the main entrance to the prison and I was escorted into an office on the left, where I was sat down. The police officer was there who'd driven me in – the other one had stayed outside and was having a cigarette with the soldiers. There was a chap there who was armed to the teeth wearing a stab vest; he looked like something out of a SWAT team. He was sitting behind the desk. He had epaulettes on and he was obviously in charge. My passport went from one desk to another desk to a photocopier machine and pretty much everywhere. He told me to remove my watch, my wedding ring, anything else and empty my pockets. To be honest, I didn't really have anything, all I had was what I was wearing: a T-shirt, a pair of boxers, my denim shorts and a pair of flip flops, that was it. Everything else was in the suitcase on the way to England. My valuables went through the X-ray machine and that was the last I saw of my stuff! My green man-bag with phone chargers, wallet, everything else, just went and that was that. I was escorted into a little room, where I was stripped down to my boxers. I was thinking, right! Here comes the prison uniform. There were two guards in there with me. They searched me and then told me to get dressed again. I put my normal clothes on, thinking that this was odd.

From there we went into the actual prison itself, where I went into this large room with a reception desk in it. I was ushered round the other side of the reception desk, where they did all my fingerprints and photos again. They took my photograph – face on, side on – and then they decided to give me my wallet back, which was a really odd thing, I thought. There was nothing in it, just a few photographs of Heidi and the kids. Little did I know how glad I would be for those photos. A guard walked me out into the corridor when they called me back and said, "Your glasses, you need your glasses". They waved my glasses case at me, so I put my glasses back on, which was great 20-20 vision. Then we walked down this really, really long corridor.

There were lots of landings off of this corridor. We got close to the end and I looked at the sign on the wall which said "M1-11". Two guards escorted me through the door and indicated for me to pick up a mattress. There were four or five tucked under the stairwell. I pulled out the first one, looked at it and it was just disgusting. I pushed that one back in and basically shuffled through the mattresses until I found one that was more acceptable than the others. They indicated for me to carry the mattress up the stairs, which I did, up four flights of stairs, or four landings. All this time they kept shouting Billy, Billy at the top of their voices.

When I got to the top floor, there was this barred gate, which they unlocked. There was a big padlock on the gate. There was a sign on the wall there that said "M1-11 Sag Terras", which I came to understand meant "the terrace", because we were right up at the top of the building, I guess. They opened the gate and as I looked inside it was quite murky, quite dark. There were a few fluorescent lights on, but it was still quite dim. There were lots of faces looking at me. There were ten other people in this cell, and then me. In I went. They closed the door and that was that. There I was. Welcome to Mugla Prison.

Chapter Two

I walked through the gate armed with my mattress, greeting my cell mates with an: "Alright lads!" It's all I could think of. This one guy had a bit of a chuckle. They guards closed the gate and I shook hands with a few of the cell mates, and then this tall lad came up to me and introduced himself as Billy and he was an English guy, so this was the Billy the guards had been shouting about. He said, ''have you had a drink, have you had anything to eat?'' I hadn't had anything at all since breakfast – I'd had no water, no food, nothing at all. I wandered a little bit further into the cell – it was really long, about twenty metres long, but only about two and a half metres wide with a sloping ceiling, like an attic. At its lowest point it was probably about a metre and a half high and at its highest point, which was just bars all down one side, it was maybe three metres high; tall on one side and short on the other, just like an attic. All I can see are just lots and lots of beds. The smell was quite pungent! It was dark, dim and gloomy, sweaty – it wasn't great.

Billy followed me down the cell and said, "Let me get you a drink of water". He produced a little glass tumbler and a bottle of water. I drank the first one, then I drank the second one, then I drank the third one. Then he said, "Do you want a packet of cigarettes?" and I said, "I don't really smoke. I use an e-cigarette, but of course they've taken that away." He said, "Just take these, you'll probably need them! If not, just use them to bribe the guards." He gave me this packet of L&M's. There was a bed frame, which was just full of stuff, right down the bottom of the cell, and a couple of the lads were indicating that I should put my mattress on there, so I did once they had cleared it. So that was where I was sleeping, which was down the other end of the cell from Billy – he was right at the gate on the left-hand side as you come in. There was a really shitty old television that was from around the 1980s, with a really fuzzy picture and all these inquisitive people looking at me. I felt like an animal in a cage. I had a quick chat with Billy for about half an hour but not a lot of it sunk in, to be honest. I was absolutely shattered, so I said, "Look, guys, I'm going to turn in, I'm going to go to bed". So that's exactly what I did, just went to bed. Laid on my mattress – there was no pillow, no blankets, no sheets, nothing like that.

That was it. I just laid there thinking what on earth has just happened, shell shocked. Lots and lots going through my head; my family . . . everything. It was just the most surreal experience ever, I'm actually in prison. This sort of thing doesn't happen to people like me. From what was really just a simple misunderstanding. I couldn't get it straight in my head that I'd been so honest and open. I'd declared these stupid coins and everything had just escalated into this. I think I had every emotion going through my head. I was terrified, I was very emotional, I was holding back the tears, I was very, very choked. I was just anxious, worried, frustrated is probably what I felt more than anything else, just complete and utter frustration. I suppose I must have nodded off at some point.

I remember waking up a couple of times in the night with people moving around, people shuffling, but to be honest I just rolled over. I was facing the wall. My bed was under the lowest point of the ceiling, so I only had a metre and a half. If I'd sat up in bed I'd crack my head open. I remember turning my back on the world, really, and thinking get some sleep and we'll sort all this rubbish out tomorrow. It was very late. That was the end of Saturday night.

On 20th of August, the Sunday, I woke up at about seven-ish. I hadn't had much sleep at all (people had been up all night). There were people screaming and crying during the night. I reached down for my bottle of water that Billy had left me and that was gone. The packet of cigarettes that Billy had given me was gone. I thought, here we go, thieving so-and-sos! The cell was quite quiet – there were a few guys up, but it was peaceful. I saw my surroundings in daylight for the first time. I wandered up, found the loo, a hole in the ground Turkish toilet. It was also under the lowest part of the ceiling, you couldn't stand up straight. It reminded me of a cupboard under the stairs. You had to crouch down to get in there. Having a number two was going to be a challenge. I had a wee and wandered up the cell towards the gate.

I discovered the place where everybody congregates is around the television. There was one guy up who was watching CNN Turk, watching the news and seeing what was going on. It was a really poor picture, no English obviously, no translation, it was just in Turkish, so it was just a case of watching the fuzzy pictures.

There was a chap, a French lad called Rubbah, who walked up the cell and came and sat beside me, he turned out to be one of the four French paedophiles – there was a little plastic outdoor table with a few broken plastic chairs. We sat and tried to talk, but his English was appalling as was my French, so it was very much hand gestures. The next thing I know is two guards running up the stairs shouting "Syem! Syem!" Then another chap gets out of bed called Meccinda and he goes around waking everybody up – it seems to be that that's his job, he wakes everybody up and it transpires that they all have to get dressed for the guards or at least cover their top half, so shorts and T-shirts are okay. You're not allowed to have your body exposed when the guards come up. This "sye" or "syem" is a roll-call. They bsically just come in and check that you're still there, you haven't managed to get out overnight and that everything's in order within the cell. This is eight o'clock every morning and then it transpires that it's also eight o'clock every night – every twelve hours, basically. You have to stand up, stand against the right-hand side, so up against the bars, all in a nice, neat, orderly line, where they come in and count you. They count to number eleven and that was that. They disappeared, all speaking in Turkish. It seems that nobody can really understand them anyway.

With that, Billy comes over and has a chat with me, gives me some toothpaste – I haven't cleaned my teeth for a couple of days. Of course, I've got no toothbrush, so I clean my teeth with my finger and a bit of toothpaste and then he showed me where the shower was, a cell within the main cell. I walked into what I guessed had been used as a cell with a barred gate. It had a pipe going up the wall, a very old mixer tap and then somebody had put half a plastic Coke bottle with holes in it and strung it up underneath this water pipe and that was the shower! The shower was cold water only and it took your breath away it was so cold. I nicked a bit of shampoo off Billy and had my first shower, which woke me up. You always feel better after a shower, albeit a freezing cold one. Billy gave me a towel, I dried myself and put my old stuff back on and then Billy appeared with a pair of T-shirt-material shorts, like jogging bottoms but shorts, and a vest T-shirt. He said you can have one to set wear while the other set is drying; it dries in seconds because of the heat up here. He was trying to tell me how things run. He explained bits and pieces, how things work, and gave me another packet of cigarettes. He said, "I've got to go back to bed because I'm pretty rubbish in the mornings," and off he went back to bed.

I just sat there – had a couple of puffs on this cigarette and then put it out and then had another couple of puffs a bit later on. I didn't really want to start smoking, but I just needed to calm myself down. Having a quick puff seemed to do the trick. The floor is concrete as are the walls which are covered in a half-arsed white-wash. It reminded me of a tigers cage back in the sixties or seventies, no room to move and animals laying in their own filth; great I'm in a zoo! I start looking round the cell for hidden cameras and microphones. This must be some sort of weird reality show. I'm expecting Ant and Dec to jump out at any time and tell me it's all a joke; surely this can't be real.

Most of the cell mates go back to bed and then about half ten-ish, they all get up, or at least the ones that are devout Muslims and pray every day – they pray five times a day. They're all Muslims of different degrees, except Billy, who's Christian, and me, of course. The praying ones, of which there were probably six or seven, they'd all get up and all have a wash behind their ears and wash their feet in particular. They had a special bucket, so they could wash their feet. Then they would all face Mecca on the prayer mats and pray.

When Billy got up he produced some loo paper and said, "It's in my locker – if you need anything out of my locker, just help yourself". Typically British, typically the sort of thing that I would do. We're there to help each other and share. He was so nice to me. He explained that there was no drinking water, but we could buy that. He joked, nothing is free here, you even have to pay for the electricity, 50 TL a month. He explained that you could order things from what they called the canteen. You obviously couldn't go down to a canteen or a shop, but you could order it on a Tuesday night on a bit of requisite paper, which you also had to buy, and they would bring it up on a Wednesday afternoon. Billy said he'd help me out with the first order if I didn't have money. That was another worry – I had not a penny on me, everything I had had been confiscated. He explained that there was no actual running water, at least not permanently. You'd have the cold water which would be turned on between eight and eight-thirty in the morning, and then twelve and one, and then six and seven every day. The prisoners would fill up old dustbins with water so that the guys that slept or the guys that didn't have a shower could have a jug wash at any point in the day. They'd also use that water for flushing the toilet and washing their clothes. They'd wash their T-shirts, their clothes with washing powder that of course you'd have to buy. You have to buy everything. The only time the hot water came on was on the Tuesday morning between 10:30- 12:00 and Friday afternoon 16:30- 18:00, where it would cause so much friction, because people would fight over the hot water. Some people would take the mickey and have a twenty minute shower, others would be half-decent and have a short shower – five minutes or so – but it would cause fights and rows, because people would want to be first in the queue and not last in the queue.

Billy explained all this to me and it was like a mass of information, really hard to digest exactly where I was, what was going on, what the procedures were. Billy went back to bed and slept until about midday. I was starving hungry, there was no breakfast supplied. There were a few bread rolls that came up, but Billy said if you eat those then you're going to be on the toilet pretty much permanently. It was a case of instant diarrhoea. The best thing to do is just hang on and lunch will arrive around twelve-ish and then you'll have your evening meal at about six-ish. He did explain that there were other things, like fruit and veg and things like that you could actually buy – nothing like that was supplied. You might get the odd bit of fruit during the day and maybe a drinking yoghurt or something, but that was pretty much it. The yoghurt and fruit should be kept in the fridge which was otherwise empty. However, if you put anything in the fridge it was 'fair game' and the chances were somebody would steal it!

When lunch arrived, which was just gone twelve, it came up in what looked like old tea urns, obviously with no tap on the side, but like a big tea urn with a lid on it. There were two of those. This really huge Arab called Medi seemed to be in charge of the food and in charge of the kitchen. I think he'd just taken on that role. He had managed to murder twenty-three women and children whilst trying to escape the Turkish coastguard and was sentenced to twenty-three years for it. A piece of work!! He had a permanent cigarette in his mouth, even when he was dishing up the food! He walked up to the gate, picked up the tea urns from the guards and then wandered back down to the kitchen area . . . I say kitchen area – there was a sink in there and a bed and that was it, there wasn't anything else in there! But it's what I guessed was an old cell, the rest was all open-plan.

He started dishing up the food. I went down there and was given a white plastic bowl, well it was white thirty years ago, now it was stained a sort of brown colour. When it was my turn my bowl was filled with a level soup ladle of rice and a level soup ladle of beans. If you can imagine baked beans with no sauce on, that's kind of exactly what it was. It was as though they'd had the sauce washed off them and just thrown on the top of the rice and that was lunch. It was a very, very meagre portion. Medi gave me my food – you were only given spoons, there were no knives and forks. They were made of metal, but honestly you could tie a knot in them they were so soft.

I was absolutely starving after lunch, still hungry, but of course there's nothing else to eat. Another huge Arab appeared, he had slept beside me. This guy was from Georgia and he seemed to take an instant dislike to me. He seemed to have a bigger portion of food than everybody else. He was very aggressive in his nature. There were only three chairs, but he would push people out and sit down and eat his lunch. He was like the school bully, I guess. He tried to move me with grunt and a shove but I refused to move. I don't think he knew what to make of me, somebody standing up to him. He did try and antagonise me and annoy me – he'd flick food and things like that at the table, just try and push my buttons, but of course I didn't react, I let him do what he had to do. I wasn't going to be bullied by him. I don't think he was used to people standing up to him.

In a cell of eleven people you've got to go in there and state your case. You can't be some wilting daisy, otherwise you're going to get treated like a wilting daisy. I went in there with a bit of front, a bit of bravado and just tried to find my place. It was like a pack of dogs or lions – you have to find your place within that group and I certainly didn't want to be down the bottom, so I stood up to everybody in the cell and found my place pretty quickly.

Billy made me a cup of coffee, which was Nescafé Classic, or at least that's what it said on the bag – it was a brown bag with a Nescafé Classic sticker on it, so I'd imagine it probably wasn't, just another Turkish knock off! Hey ho, it tasted like coffee! Billy and I chatted pretty much all afternoon. We were both motorbike crazy – I've been a biker for years, so has Billy, so we had a lot in common. I've got the boys – at that time they were eight and nine. Billy had girls, he had a girl who was eight and then two little ones, three and four. We had loads in common other than just being British.

Billy had a small fencing business which he'd built up from scratch and was very proud of. He showed me some photos his wife had printed and sent in; pictures of his family, his bikes and his cars. They portrayed a very normal, down to earth kind of guy, a family man with lovely wife and three gorgeous children.

There was a lot to talk about, a lot to catch up on. Billy had had no contact with the outside world for a long time. He was arrested on April 11th 2017 and we're now towards the end of August, so there was an awful lot that Billy hadn't heard or he'd had no news of. We just chatted pretty much all afternoon. He told me how things worked within the cell, within the prison. If you needed things then you'd have to ask the manager or the Bash Mahmoud, as he was known in Turkish, or the warden I guess, in English. You'd have to ask, and you'd have to submit a written letter in Turkish to get your request through so that you could actually go and see him. He explained to me that you would have to ask the guy on the landing below, who was a Daesh or ISIS terrorist called Ali – he had half-decent Turkish. He was a Belgian lad, but he had reasonable Turkish and he could write the letter for you for a price of two cigarettes, so you'd send two cigarettes down on a bit of string and then he'd send the letter back up. Hold the boat, a Daesh terrorist, two cigarettes for a letter?? Just what the hell kind of place was I in?

During the afternoon and the evening, I met the rest of the cell mates. Of course, I instantly liked Billy, we got on really, really well, and then a chap they called the Captain. He was the Captain of the ship which was caught by the Turkish Coastguard off the coast of Libya with two and a half tons of Hashish on board, however I got on really well with him too. Captain was a very quiet man, kept himself to himself. He was no trouble, only spoke a very small amount of English, but he seemed to be quite a nice guy. He was an older gentleman – fifty-seven or fifty-eight – but he was okay, I got on alright with him. Billy was an Essex lad and he had a terrible story which I'll touch on later.

I learned most of these people's stories through Billy. Some of them had awful stories. When I started to learn just who these guys were and what they were in for, I kind of had an impending sense of doom. Four French paedophiles, sentenced to sixteen years each, a murderer that had killed twenty-three women and children, sentenced to twenty-three years, a human trafficker, awaiting sentencing, an armed robber, not yet sentenced, a thief with six years, two drug smugglers, twenty years each and that was just my cell. On the landing below were four Daesh or Isis terrorists, four or five murderers, and the Executioner, who had shot a policeman in the face, killing him. This piece of work had got thirty-five years! On the landing below them, were forty seven Feto terrorists, all awaiting sentencing. I was in a cell with these guys who were seriously hardened criminals and all I'd done was declare a few coins at the airport. I felt just so frustrated and so helpless, absolutely terrified, my head was spinning.

About half past two that afternoon, Billy explained that there was an activity called Barsha, just for the people from our cell only. We're not aloud to have any contact with any prisoners outside our cell. I'm laughing when I say it, because it's just crazy. The guards come up and ask if anybody wants to go down to the Barsha, so me thinking a bit of exercise, a bit of sunshine, out in the exercise yard would be great. We walked down the four flights of stairs, a few of the cell mates go down, and we were escorted to what was called an outside area, but it's not an outside area, it's like a room with fifteen metre high walls, barbed wire across the top, it's just got no ceiling, just barbed wire. It's the hottest place I've ever been. I don't know how many degrees it was, but you walked into it and you were instantly soaked with sweat. The heat in there was unbelievable. People were all scrabbling for the shade and I'm thinking, Tobe, what the hell are you doing out here? This room was only four metres by four metres and it was like a hell-hole. It must have been forty plus degrees in there. I was drowning in my own sweat.

I banged on the door and a guard appeared and I indicated that I wanted to go back up upstairs. He just laughed at me and said, "One hour, one hour". I was like, you mean I have to wait here for an hour, I can't go back upstairs? "One hour, one hour." So that was that. The hour came and went and we were all escorted back up. At which point I jumped straight into the shower area and had a jug wash and then thankfully put on Billy's shorts and vest top that he'd given me and spent ten minutes or so washing out my clothes that I'd come in with.

At around six-ish dinner turned up, yet again rice and beans. Vlad the Impaler, (Kasabian song) as I'd called him, the guy sleeping next to me, the huge Arab guy, he tried to push my buttons again; took a lot of the food and then he sits at the table trying to force me to move, but I didn't budge, I kept my cool. He just tried to antagonise me all the time by pushing his bowl into mine and standing on my feet under the table etc. At eight o'clock a few more people appeared and got out of bed – some had slept all day – and they all came down towards the TV and it transpires that at about eight o'clock every night, on Turkish TV – I can't remember the channels – but on one of the channels, there's always a film, so we ended up watching Batman in Turkish, which was the most surreal thing ever. Watching Heath Ledger speaking Turkish was just a head-spin!

This went on until about ten thirty. Then I spoke to Billy – he said he needed to see the doctor, he wanted to get some sleeping tablets and I hadn't slept really at all, so I said I'll join him and we'd get a letter written. We spoke to Ali, the lad below, the terrorist lad, and he wrote us a letter, so we had to give him four cigarettes, because it was two letters, and then we put the finished letters in the little plastic container which is tied on the cell gate for the morning where the guards collect all the paperwork at Syem.

At about eleven o'clock or so, I just said I'm going to hit the sack and that was that. Off I went to jolly old bed again, still no bed clothes or anything like that. It got quite cold in the evening. There were some windows on the far side, three long windows, you could only see the sky out of them, but they were on the other side of the bars. They were about three or four metres away from us, but when there was a breeze . . . during the day it was quite nice, but at night it got really cold. Of course, you've got no blankets or anything, so you just lay in bed freezing and worrying about everything.

Chapter Three

<u>Monday 21st</u>

I get up just after seven, really, really tired. I haven't had much sleep at all. A couple of the lads are up, some of them praying. There's one guy in particular, on the landing below, who they call The Executioner – he's directly below me and he chooses to pray, he chooses to sing, but he's got one of those booming voices that is just so loud, like a jet engine. It's a vast, open area and even the slightest sound seems to be amplified by ten. The Executioner has no consideration for anybody else and sings for hours on end through the day and night, followed up with a prayer. Horrible, horrible man. I'm very, very tired now and the sleep deprivation is beginning to take its toll. I walked down towards the television, CNN Turk's on yet again.

The bottom door opens, which is four floors below me. Lots of guards come in, probably twenty plus, and they get all of Feto terrorists out of their cells. They're all being searched, they've all got paperwork with them, which is also being sifted through. I don't really understand what's going on. I asked one of the lads and he tells me that they're all terrorists and they're all going to macaman, which is Turkish for "court". He tries to explain, as best he can, that they're Feto terrorists. I'd read about these guys and that they had tried to kill Erdoğan, the Turkish president and overthrow the government back in the summer of 2016 in what can only be described as a military coup. They're all loyal to what used to be Erdoğan's right-hand man, a guy called Fethullah Gülen, hence the Feto nickname. Out of the thousands of soldiers, judges and school teachers arrested, there were forty-seven soldiers in custody, three floors below me. In short, they had used helicopter gunships, tanks and various military weapons to take over Istanbul and attack and kill Erdogan in Marmaris when he was on holiday, but in doing so I believe they had killed over 300 innocent people and injured many more. Erdogan, somehow had managed to escape, and later ordered the mass arrests.

These soldiers, Feto terrorists, were all that remained after the arrests and were in Mugla prison awaiting sentencing, the supposed ring leaders. Apparently, this is why the prison is guarded from the outside too, explaining why I had seen the heavy military presence outside when I arrived. The lads tell me they go to court pretty much every day, it's an ongoing thing. There's talk of Turkey bringing back the death sentence and hanging all these guys. A few of these lads look up and give us the nod but are soon reprimanded by the guards.

After they leave for court the guards come up for usual eight o'clock, syem. We all stand up and get counted. Then they leave and a short while later, two guards come up to the gate and call my name. They've got a photographer with them. I'm escorted out onto the landing outside the cell where they explain: "Photo . . . ID." I believe this is a prison ID, everyone has to have one. The guards gesture to me to hold this board up in front of my chest and face the photographer. I notice that the spelling of my name was wrong. My middle name is John and they've got it as Jonh. I point this out, so they put me back in the cell and disappear. A short while later, they come back again with it still spelt the wrong way! I give up, yep, whatever. I hold this board up and they take pictures of me – front, back, sides – then when I put the board down to go back in the cell, they stop me and ask me to take my T-shirt off. I take my T-shirt off and then they proceeded to photograph my tattoos. I reckon that this is in case, by the remotest of chances I escape, then they have extra chances at identifying me! They also took a photograph of my hand, because I've got a couple of fingers missing on the left hand. Then back in the cell I go.

Half an hour or so later, the guards reappear and say, "Bash Mahmoud", which is the manager. Obviously, I'm going down to see him. They tell me I have to get dressed. Well, I'm wearing shorts and T-shirt which is the only thing I own and, but they say I must have long trousers. So, I explained to them with help from the other cell mates that I haven't got any and that this is what I came with. The debate went on for five minutes or so before they gave in. Anyway, I went down in my shorts and T-shirt.

At the bottom of the landing you go into this huge corridor. There was a table there with a small man, bald, just instant dislike, strange little guy, surrounded by his lackies. I had managed to take a prisoner down with me called Medi, who had some English and some Turkish, as a translator. He knew what I wanted, A, to see a doctor, B, to see the consul and C, I wanted a telephone call to my wife. Medi explained all these things. He just flicked his hand and shooed us both away, like he was shooing away a fly! I tried to carry on the conversation, but the guards grabbed hold of me and moved me back up the corridor towards M1-11 where I climbed the stairs and went back into the cell. When I quizzed Medi about what had happened, he just said oh it's nothing, you don't get anything here. Okay, so that's where we are, a complete waste of time and yet more frustration.

At lunchtime, Vlad took all the food yet again and unfortunately, I was the last man in the kitchen, so when I got my bowl and stood there looking expectantly at Medi, *can I have some food please?* there was none left. So, I walked up to the cell with a spoon and an empty bowl, looked at Vlad's plate which was overflowing and proceeded to take half of his food and put it on my plate, which didn't go down too well, to say the least! I thought he was going to blow a fuse. But I stood my ground and ate my food, while he sat opposite me fuming.

After lunch, I got some paper from Billy and I wrote a letter to Heidi and the boys, which was very emotional, to say the least. I popped it in an envelope and then stuck it in the plastic holder on the gate ready for the morning.

That afternoon, the lads put the TV on a popular Turkish channel called Kral Pop. This is basically the top twenty Turkish pop songs, it goes on and on and on. It's like the Eurovision Song Content over and over and over again. I'm already beginning to hate it, it's far from the music that I like. Just on repeat all the time. It was tedious.

About two-ish, Vlad went off to take a shower and as he came out my towel was hanging on the bars just outside the shower drying. He picked up my towel and dried himself with it, all the time looking at me as if to say what are you going to do about it? I didn't react, I left it alone, and he just left the towel in a heap on the floor. So I went and picked it up, hung it up and went back and sat down at the table again wondering what I should do about his direct provocation. I kept mulling over and mulling over in my mind – what should I do about it, I'm still trying to establish my place within this group and so far I had shown no signs of backing down to anyone.

A couple of hours later, I thought well, here's goes nothing. I went and had a shower, or a jug wash, after which I wandered up the cell stark naked, which was quite a shock for some of the lads. Vlad was sitting at the table in plain sight. I picked up his prayer mat and dried myself with it, bollocks and all, all the time holding eye contact with him. He reacted in what can only be described as like a cartoon character reaction with steam coming out of his ears! It was quite funny really. I thought that Billy was going to bust a gut laughing! I honestly thought Vlad was going to go for me there and then, but he didn't. I then turned leaving his prayer mat in a heap on the floor and went to get dressed.

The evening was the same as every other evening, film and then I went to bed. Still couldn't sleep. Really, really tired, over-tired. Everything going on in my head, thinking about so many things and yet the constant noise – people crying and praying.

It must have been two in the morning or so when The Executioner started singing and that was it, the final straw for me. I got out of my bed and walked over to the bars and shouted down at him. I basically told him to shut the fuck up to which he replied, "I kill you, English. I kill you, English," then he started singing at the top of his voice even louder than before. What could I do to shut this guy up? I stood by the bars for a while, then for some strange reason I sung the National Anthem as loud as I possibly could. It seemed to do the trick, he went quiet, I went quiet, and then I heard a little "I kill you English" and that was the end of that. So I went back to bed and must have finally nodded off.

On the Tuesday I woke up and grabbed myself a coffee from Billy's locker, went and sat down and watched the pictures on CNN Turk and as you do. Out of the corner of my eye I saw Vlad doing something underneath my bed. I was thinking to myself what are you doing under there? Really sneaky. I waited until he'd gone and looked underneath the bed. Where the head of the bed meets the side of the bed, somebody had welded on a little rectangle of metal – as a strengthener, I guess – and on there he'd put a pack of playing cards. Now these playing cards were basically the backs of cigarette packets that had been torn off and made into playing cards. The prisoners had then drawn on the two of diamonds, three of diamonds and so on with a biro. I had seen Vlad playing cards with the French lads during the evenings. Knowing now that the French lads were sex offenders I steered clear of them as best I could in the confined space that we all shared!!

Billy had already told me that if you get caught with any kind of gambling stuff – cards or anything at all – you get an extra six months on your sentence and that will be in solitary confinement. I started to get a little bit worried, because the cells get turned over a couple of times a week. The guards come rushing up the stairs on mass and basically take you outside the cell onto the landing, where they just turn everything over inside. They're looking for whatever they need to look for, I guess. Then you're allowed back in to tidy up. I was really quite anxious about the cards underneath my bed, but I didn't let on that I knew they were there.

Vlad is continuously bullying this guy, Seka, I think his real name is Serkan, but everybody calls him Seka. He's a very simple and childish man. I would imagine his mental age or capacity is around that of a ten-year-old. However, he's thirty-four. He's an armed robber from Azerbaijan. He's quite a gentle soul really and quite likeable. He's a bit like a Jack Russell puppy – he's full on and then he sleeps, generally he just wants to please you all the time but can become a bit annoying none the less. But Vlad just keeps bullying him, hitting him and slapping him, pushing him about and throwing his weight around, picking on the weakest member of the pack.

At half past ten-ish, the hot water comes on and I get into the shower finally and it's just heaven. It puts me back in the place where I want to be. It washes away all the filth, the grime, even some of the memories of what's going on in my head, experiences and things, it just makes you feel clean. It was absolutely fantastic.

Lunch was lunch, same old – rice and beans – and then at about one o'clock I was asked to go down to see the manager yet again. I went down to see the manager and he wanted to know what I wanted the previous day. Seriously confused now, but with Medi in tow again, I explained that I needed to see the British consul. He made a note of it and I thought perhaps he was actually going to do something about it, happy days! I was separated from Medi who escorted back up the corridor and up to the cell. The manager disappeared down the corridor in the opposite direction.

I was left with two guards who walked me to small room at the bottom of my landing in which I hadn't been in before. I was forcefully pushed into the room and the big metal door was slammed shut behind me. There was another prisoner in there, great big fella in his middle thirties. I had no idea what was going on. I didn't know who he was or anything. The door was bolted behind us – it was a very small cell, no CCTV, no cameras, there was just a plastic chair in the room and that was it, just me and this this fella standing there. He took one look at me and he said, "I kill you, English," and I thought oh my God! Here we go! This is The Executioner. I had come to learn that this guy was Georgian mafia and had shot a policeman in the face, killing him. I immediately tried to talk my way out of the inevitable. I said to him, "Look, I don't want any trouble with you, I just want a bit of peace and quiet at night." There was no telling him, he wouldn't listen to anything, and I don't suppose he had much English anyway. So I turned round and showed my back to him to show basically that I don't fear you, but I also want to get out of here, because you're a lot bigger than me and bloody scary too.

I banged on the cell door and as I did so he punched me in the back of the head. The guards came to the door, they opened the hatch, like an inspection hatch, they looked at me, laughed and closed it. So I thought, oh, you're on your own, Tobe. I took my glasses off, my watch off that I'd only just got back – I bribed one of the guards ten cigarettes to get my watch back, and five cigarettes for my wedding ring! I then took my T-shirt off and I gestured to him. I said, "Right, if this has got to happen then take your T-shirt off." As he pulled his T-shirt up over his head, I knew this was my only chance of catching him off guard, I just went for him. While his head and arms were still tied up in his T-shirt, I kicked him straight in the bollocks and punched him in the throat, he just doubled up and went down. I remember jumping on top of him, just sitting on top of him, just punching and punching and punching. His hands and his arms are all still all caught up in his T-shirt as I continued, just punching his head through this T-shirt. There was blood everywhere. Then everything becomes a blur.

The next thing I remember is the two guards holding my arms, restraining me, pulling me off of him while I was screaming, "Get the fuck off me!" I had so much adrenaline and I was shaking like a leaf with all this adrenaline pumping round my body. A different guard appeared, this one had epaulettes on, so he's slightly more senior, I guess. He sat me on the bottom of the stairs on the stairwell up to our landing. There's a sink there opposite the stairs, he said, "Wait, you wait". So, I sat there, shaking like a jelly, just in my shorts, covered in blood, looking down at my hands which are already swelling up. He took the two guards that had brought me into the room initially, back into the room where The Executioner was, and boy did he shout at them. Finally, they were dismissed and then maybe four or five guards turned up and proceeded to carry The Executioner out of the room. They disappeared back into the corridor, I don't know where they went.

This senior guard introduced himself as Mahmood. He got some paper towels and blue roll, soaked in water and helped me clean myself up. Then he went back into the room and got my T-shirt and my watch and glasses. He said, "You wait, you wait." So I waited there and calmed down, all the time Mahmood standing there, watching over me. Eventually, I got dressed and I suppose I must have been there twenty minutes, at least. I remember running my hands underneath the cold tap for ages, to keep the swelling down and they were really quite painful. Eventually, he took me up to the cell and I just went in. I never said anything to anybody. I took my shorts off, there was a bit of blood on them, but before anybody could see it I put them in a washing-up bowl with some cold water to get the blood out and then I put on my shorts that I'd washed previously in the hot shower. I just sat pretty quietly for the rest of the day. I was so ashamed of what I'd done, because in my job on the ambulance I help people, not beat them to a pulp. I was ashamed at just how far I had gone, perhaps this is the 'red mist' people talk about. I'm not a violent person, but I suppose when my back was against the wall it was the only way out. I felt guilt, I felt shame, but I didn't really know what to feel. I was trying to justify what had happened over and over in my head. I found it really, really hard to justify it. I didn't want to talk to anybody about it, I wanted to put it in the back of my mind and bottle it up.

Finally, I went to bed around ten or eleven o'clock. I was lying in bed and I heard this funny noise. I couldn't figure out what it was. It was coming from outside the cell towards where the windows were. I looked over and there was this tiny little owl – I couldn't really see it properly, but it was really tiny. Where the fluorescent lights were on, you could just see these huge eyes. My wife is crazy about owls and I thought wow! What an omen. It's a message from my wife. I got really emotional. It really touched me. I finally nodded off and that was the end of Tuesday.

At about three in the morning, Wednesday, one of the lads, Meccinda came and woke me up. He told me in broken English, he said, "Seka! He's dead! Seka's dead! Seka's hanging!" What the hell, what?! So confused, when you wake up from that sleep and you don't know what's going on. He said, "He's dead, you come, you come. Quick, quick!" I shot up out of bed and ran up the cell, there were a couple of other lads there and they were getting him down from the top of the bars. He'd basically climbed the bars, put his elastic belt round his neck and hung himself. They got him down and managed to lay him on his back on the concrete floor. After a struggle, I managed to get his elastic belt off his neck. I can't feel the pain in my hands at all, must be the adrenaline. He had no pulse, not breathing, dead as a dodo. I said, "How long? How long's he been there?" They reckoned five minutes maybe, they didn't know. I checked for an open airway and there was no airway, the belt had seen to that. His throat had collapsed where the belt had tightened around his wind pipe, which was basically just squashed. I spent what felt like ten minutes, but it was probably only a few seconds, trying to manipulate this airway, trying to get his windpipe, his trachea, back into shape. I said to Billy, "Billy, go and get that bit of pipe off the tap on the sink, the little green one." It was all I could think of. So Billy shot off and went and got the hose pipe. I continued massaging his windpipe and just as Billy came with the hosepipe, it just popped and out it came, back into shape. I had a quick feel and it was good, relief, we had an airway, so I jumped straight on his chest and started compressions. Within a couple of minutes, I didn't do many compressions at all, he was breathing again, and I had a strong pulse in his neck. Shortly afterwards, he opened his eyes, gasping for breath. I suppose within about five minutes he was back sitting on his bed.

He was pretty croaky, but he was talking and back in the room. The guys had already pressed the alarm outside the cell for the guards to come up, but they never attended, so to this day none of the guards, the prison system, no one knows that poor old Seka tried to take his life. Crazy times, crazy times. This place is a crazy zoo but for tonight at least, peace is restored. I wander back down the cell and get back to bed wondering what would have happened if I hadn't been there. Would Seka have died, would somebody else have got him back? So many unanswered questions.

We wake up in the morning, same old story, syem and all the usual. About nine-ish I hear all these footsteps on the stairs coming up and I know full well what's happening. We're going to get rumbled. Quick as you like, I ran down towards my bed, got the playing cards and just threw them in Vlad's pillow case. He slept beside me so it was just a case of throwing them in. About twenty guards arrived with the same number of gendarme, all armed to the teeth with what look like AKs – they had the works – all showing this massive force of strength. A bit puerile really, but hey ho! We all got marched out of the cell onto the landing at the top of the stairs. You can see through the gate, they're turning mattresses over and pulling things off walls, going through people's lockers.

I suppose about ten minutes later, a couple of guards come out with Vlad's pillow case and that's him done, escorted away. Never saw the bloke again. However, life was an awful lot easier without him. There was a sense of relief, I think, from everybody in the cell. I felt a bit guilty about what I'd done, but it was another case of him or me. Fortunately, I'd seen what he'd done and where he was hiding the cards and in this instance, it was him, so off he went. Never saw him again. He didn't go to the solitary cells underneath us, so I've no idea where he went. But that was the end of Vlad the Impaler.

There was a big shuffle around with beds, because now there's a spare bed beside me and everybody's moving around. This creates a spare bed beside Billy. What we do is we put Seka right next to Billy, because Billy stays up quite late, so he can keep an eye on him. Seka's got this weird affinity with Billy – he's always hanging around Billy, always smiling, always trying to please Billy, so we figure that if we put him beside Billy, it might increase his confidence and his well-being, which proved to be the case, to be fair.

At about half past three that afternoon, the canteen arrives and Billy, bless him, has got me some bits and pieces, which I didn't ask for, so out of the kindness of his heart, out of his own meagre providings, his money, he'd got me a toothbrush, some shampoo, some deodorant and a couple of packets of cigarettes, which was lovely. I spent the afternoon and that evening cleaning my teeth! I think I must have cleaned them 'til my gums were on fire, they were bleeding I remember! It was a great feeling to actually clean my teeth properly and not use my finger any more, it was fantastic.

It wasn't a bad day, in those respects. I wrote a letter to Mum – I call her Mumsie, but she's really my mother-in-law – she's great, I was missing her. I then wrote a letter to my brother and sister-in-law, on Heidi's side. I wanted to write but I think mainly because I needed to occupy my time, time was really, really dragging in here. There was nothing to do. There was a television that gave you a headache if you watched it for more than two hours at a time because of the fuzzy picture. Some days were better than others. Other than that, there was nothing else to do. There were a few old magazines. Billy had a few bike magazines, which I'd already read cover to cover. He had a few *Top Gear* magazines too, but basically there was nothing else. All the other reading material was in Arabic – it was the Koran and prayer books. There was absolutely nothing to do. I occupied my time as best I could, zoning out for the most part.

I went and had a shower and discovered Timotei! I had visions of the advert years ago – with a blonde girl in the waterfall and I thought this is going to be nice! I'm going to wash my body and my hair and get myself nice and clean, but this Timotei was burning my skin, particularly around my eyes, it was really red. Billy said, "What have you done?" I said, "I've only just had a shower." He said, "Ahh, they copy everything in Turkey! You only have to look at the coffee." With that he peeled the label off and underneath it was *shampoo* in Arabic or something, some dodgy, hooky make! They'd just put a Timotei sticker over the top, more Turkish knock off's! So, I didn't use that shampoo again. That was pretty much it for Wednesday.

Thursday morning, same old story. However, at nine in the morning, the guards came up to the gate. I was sitting there wondering what they wanted, and a guard called out the four

French lads' names, he calls out Billy's name, and Billy says, "Oh, it's for the phone call, we get a phone call on a Thursday at nine in the morning". And then low and behold, they call out my name and Billy says, "Tobe! Tobe! You've got a phone call! Have you got a phone card?" "No, of course I haven't got a phone card!" Billy manages to persuade one of the French lads to give me a spare card. So, armed with a phone card, I follow the others down, bouncing off the walls I'm so excited.

As we reach the bottom of the stairs, the lads all know the routine, there's some payphones in the corridor and they all go and find a payphone. Mahmood comes over, the guy that had helped me after the fight, he said, "Come! Come!" So, I went with him and he showed me into another landing with lots of cells off it, just off the main corridor, where there was a payphone on the wall. He explained as best he could how to do it. He put the card in for me. He had a bit of paper with a phone number on it, which was my wife's phone number. He dialled it but no joy, it wouldn't work. Yet again, another frustration. Mahmood told me, "You wait," and then he went off. On his return we tried again then. "Wait, wait!" He went to and fro several times and then finally, on about the fourth attempt it started ringing and my heart was just in my mouth.

I couldn't believe that, what's been a week now since I've seen my wife and talked to my wife and heard their voices, I was finally going to speak to them. With that Heidi picked up the phone and probably for about the first, I don't know, it felt forever, but I suppose for about the first three or four minutes we were crying and really, really emotional. Asking each other loads of questions: How are you? What are you doing? What's going on? Finally, we pull it together and Heidi explains to me that my appeal that they'd lodged was actually happening today, Thursday. There was me thinking why wasn't I there? Why wouldn't I be there? Heidi didn't have any answers. Normally I'd expect to be at my own appeal, but who knew? She also told me that I was going to see the British consul on Friday, tomorrow, who was coming to the prison to see me. This gave me a huge sense of relief, that people were working behind the scenes, that people were working really hard to get me out, that they were doing all they could. Heidi was saying we're doing everything we can. I said, "Heids, you've got to get me out of here. This place is crazy." She said to me, "Have you had any trouble? Are they nice to you? Are they bad to you?" "Look, Heids, it's glasses off, watch off, and windmill time." I think she knew exactly what I meant, but she didn't push it any further. I said don't worry about me, I'm okay, I can deal with everything in here. I explained that all the other lads, when they come to attack you, they fight with flip flops – for some reason that's one of their biggest insults that they can offer you is to hit you with flip flops or their shoes. When you turn around and punch them, they're completely surprised and shocked that you've taken that amount of violence to them. I explained, I'm an English guy, I don't fight with flip flops! This bought a bit of a light relief to our otherwise very emotional conversation. I remember telling them I loved them, I spoke to the boys, it was all on speaker, and it was wonderful, absolutely amazing. I was still talking when the phone went dead.

Ten minutes, that's all you get and then you're just cut off. I was annoyed that the phone call had finished, but I was so elated, I was buzzing. I was so happy that things were happening, people were helping me and that I'd had the chance to speak to my wife. At the end of the phone call, I took the card out the machine and walked back down the corridor, where Mahmood called me over and said, "Sign, sign," and it was obviously a thing to say that you'd received a phone call. It had *telephone* written on it, so I was happy to sign. I ended up shaking Mahmood's hand and giving him a man hug. I remember saying thank you, thank you, thank you for letting me talk to my wife. It was amazing, absolutely amazing. For the rest of that day I was absolutely buzzing.

Friday comes and I'm very excited. The British consul's coming to see me. I'm really, really excited. I feel that things are happening, and the consul are here to help me out now. Half past ten, the guards come up and call my name. They tell me to put long trousers on and I explain I haven't got long trousers. I walk down and I end up in this little manager's office, the one that had shooed me away. I was sitting there and I crossed my legs, but because I had one of my feet in the air, he gestured to me to put my foot down. I didn't know if I was offending him, if it was an Arab thing or what it was, I didn't know. I put my foot down and waited. Soon enough, the British consul came in – a lady – we shook hands and following her was a little prisoner, obviously a trustee, and he brought some tea in . . . for everybody except me! I said to the British consul, "Ahh, I'll have a tea please." She turned to the prisoner and said, "Can I have one more tea please?" in Turkish. The prisoner looked at the warden, who didn't really know what to do with himself, but finally gave in. Ten minutes later I had a cup of tea, which was nice, a win for the little guy, or so it felt. Only Turkish chai, but better than nothing.

We chatted and chatted. She gave me loads and loads of paperwork, which unfortunately was confiscated at the end of the meeting and I didn't end up seeing that for about another two to three weeks. It all had to be translated, so anything useful that might have been in it was pointless. I realised that some of the prisoners had jobs. Thinking that this may help to pass the time I asked if I could work in the sick bay as I had some medical experience. ''No Turkish, no work'', that's all he said. I came away from that meeting thinking, well, what was the point in that? I didn't really get much out of it at all. However, the British consul did manage to put £75 into my prison account, so that I could use that to buy toiletries and requisites from the canteen. Heidi had given them the money by electronic transfer. I also managed to secure an appointment for Billy and myself to see the doctor that afternoon. I don't think I would have got that unless the consul was there. It was all good news in that respect.

I was met by Mahmood's desk when the meeting ended and there were a couple of the French guys from my cell there. I don't know what they were doing there. We all walked back up to the cell together. As we were walking up, The Executioner was walking down. Honestly, he looked like hell, he really did. As he walked past me, he turned and punched me in the back of the head! The guards grabbed hold of him immediately and I grabbed him by the throat. I just didn't let go. Eventually, he dropped on his knees and I said to him, "You don't fucking learn do you, mate?" I let go and just carried on walking up the stairs. I think the guards were a bit shocked. A couple of the French guys had seen what I'd done and they were shocked too. They were like, "Whooah, Toby! Strong man, strong man! Yeah! Toby!" We get up to the cell and now everybody's talking about what I did to The Executioner, which was pretty crazy. I played it down and refused to talk about it. From then on the lads started calling me Bubba, which means big brother. Either that or Mr Toby, the guards started calling me Mr Toby! Which I found pretty mad and amusing!

That afternoon Billy and I go and see the doctor. Outside the doctor's office there's a set of scales, so Billy and I both jump on the scales. Billy's thirteen stone eleven and he's worried he's lost loads of weight. I'm nothing like that – I'm fifteen stone thirteen! I'm huge! It must have been the holiday – all-you-can eat and all-inclusive buffets. We go in there and see the doctor separately. Billy comes out and he says, "Oh, great, I've got some sleeping tablets, so that's going to help me sleep. I can't wait to sleep." I go in and I get sleeping tablets too. He said, "Do I have any more medical problems?" "No, no, I'm good." So with that, yes, you can have sleeping tablets and off we go. We get a month's prescription for sleeping tablets. No tablets yet, but he said in a couple of days when it goes through the system they'll bring them up to us. I go back to the cell, write yet more letters to my oldest three kids, Zoe, Zach and Victoria.

Chapter Four

<u>Saturday morning</u>

I get out of bed and go and get my coffee. My hands are getting much better now – the swelling's going down – and I can hold my coffee cup with one hand, rather than the two! A bit of progress there. Seka wakes up as well and a few of the other lads, It's becoming more and more noticeable that poor old Seka's getting bullied. They're picking on him and teasing him, just generally trying to antagonise him and work him up into a frenzy, for their own amusement. I have a word with them and basically say, "Look, lads, it's gotta stop, you've gotta leave it out." They seem to listen to me now, these lads, these prisoners, they take it on board and I notice over the day that it calms down a bit. They still niggle him a bit, but generally it's getting better. Not much else happens on Saturday. The weekends are quiet. There are no people going down to see doctors or wardens or anything. It's generally the worst time, because you're just confined to your cell and nothing happens.

However just sitting by the telly, my eyes get pulled towards the power socket behind the tv. The two wires from the tv are just pushed into the socket, no plug!! With nothing else to do I wander round the cell looking at the electrics. The whole cell is run off an extension lead plugged in just outside the cell. There are two tv's, one down by the French lads which they have bought and is exclusive to them, two fans, a kettle and a fridge all running off one socket!? The fans are spliced into the cable itself!? The Fire Brigade would have field day in here. Health a safety would shut the place down.

<u>Sunday</u>

Pretty much exactly the same. Billy and I chat for the afternoon. We get his magazines out, his *Top Gear* magazines, his *Fast Bike* magazines, and we're just chatting through, like two blokes down the pub really. Billy's a Mercedes C63 man and he likes the Ducati 1299, whereas I'm more of a down to earth Nissan Duke kind of guy! The bike I like is a Kawasaki Z1000SX, but only in orange of course! It's the newer version of my old 2006 Kawasaki Z750S. Sunday nights are quite dead. There are no films on a Sunday night, so we end up watching some sitcom in Turkish. Some of the lads seem to enjoy it, but I just look at the pictures and zone out. I did write a few more letters though, to friends and family and that was about it for Sunday.

<u>Monday 28th</u>

Woke up as usual; coffee, watched the terrorists, the 47 Feto lads off to court yet again. I was watching the CNN Turk coverage on the television while I was having my coffee. There was a big article about these 47 lads and the news were saying, or I assumed they were saying, something about a T-shirt that had *Hero* written on it. It was quite a big thing. I was talking to a couple of the lads when they woke up about it and they were saying that somebody had sent in a white T-shirt with *Hero* written on it and that one of the Feto prisoners/terrorists had worn this *Hero* T-shirt to court for two weeks, before somebody realised what it actually meant in English. Now, apparently, if you are seen to be wearing a T-shirt with the word *Hero* on it in Turkey, you're sentenced to three months in prison, no questions. If you're going to Turkey, for goodness' sake, don't put a *Hero* T-shirt on! There was a case on the television they were talking about where a chap, a foreign national, had 'Zero to Hero' written on his T-shirt. He got three months in prison, so don't wear a *Hero* T-shirt!

The usual lads come down with me to see the manager. We all get escorted down the stairwell of M1-11 and at the bottom of the steps, opposite the sink, there's a little bin and I happen to just glance out of the corner of my eye and all the letters that I'd been writing were in there, torn up, all the envelopes – I could see my own handwriting. I grabbed them out and the guard took them off me and put them back in the bin. "What's going on? What's going on?" "No English, no English." That's all I ever heard, that and "Procedure." So, I joined the back of the queue to see the manager. Everybody is ahead of me, so I'm waiting my time. I'm fuming, absolutely fuming inside. All my messages, all my emotions, all my frustrations, everything has been put in the bin. I waited 'til everybody had seen the manager and then stood there in front of him, fuming. I asked him why my letters were put in the bin. Nobody of course could speak English, so I grabbed one of the guys who had some Turkish and said translate this for me. So, he translated it and I got this ridiculous answer back that all letters have to be in Turkish so that they can be read by the guards. There's no translator apparently. I explained that my wife doesn't read Turkish! It was just unbelievable. I basically exploded. I started shouting at him, I'm banging the table, I was swearing, I was fuming, absolutely fuming. It was just so frustrating, and farcical.

The guards grabbed me straight away and walked me to the Barsha area, where I was pushed in there on my own. I presumed I was put in there to cool down. Next thing I know, ten or twelve guards come in and they surround me. I'm thinking oh my God! I'm going to get a kicking because I had an argument with the manager. By this stage, I just don't care, so glasses off, watch off, hey ho, it's windmill time! I've just put all my stuff down on the ground when Mahmood, bless him, comes storming into the Barsha area. He grabs hold of me, picks up my stuff and says, "Come with me, come, come". Yet again he sits me on the bottom of the stairs and calms me down. After a few minutes I see all the guards walking out of the Barsha and I'm escorted back up to my cell. No more explanations, that's it, back to your cell.

I decided to write another letter to see the manager. I was in one of those bolshy moods. I haven't finished with this. I want to have it out again. I asked Ali, the Daesh terrorist beneath me, if he could write me a letter to see the manager. He wrote me a letter and while he was there I asked him for one for the doctor. He sent one of those up too, so I sent him down four cigarettes. So I pretty much spent my afternoon copying the letters so I had templates. Now Meccinda had fair Turkish, so I asked him to write a few of these letters and he became everybody's scribe; I nicknamed him The Scribe. So if anybody needed to see managers or doctors for anything at all, we had these letters as templates and basically it wouldn't cost us any more cigarettes because Meccinda didn't smoke. The only one that wasn't happy about it was Ali, because he wasn't getting free cigarettes!

That evening, the Captain, bless him, had learned to ask me for a coffee. So rather than going into my locker and stealing the coffee, he would actually come up to me just before the film. Firstly, he started by saying, "Toby, is it okay if I take a coffee?" And then later on, "Can I take a coffee, and would you like one too?" It was like a eureka moment, a breath of fresh air, that these guys were actually learning to share. I suppose they'd never really done it before, but they were learning to share with me. I guess because I was trusting them, and they were getting tired of being slapped. It was a great release and a great relief for everybody.

Yassar, his brother-in-law, he was the owner of the ship that was smuggling the drugs, the two and a half tonnes of hashish, he cottoned on to what was going on. Yassar reminded me a lot of Jafar from the old Aladdin films – very sneaky and conniving, you didn't trust him at all. He started asking me for coffee when he woke up at about half past ten. He would ask me for a coffee and then make me one too. It was all very refreshing.

That evening, the sleeping tablets finally turned up, both for me and for Billy. Strangely enough we both had two different tablets, but we take them straight after the film, so about ten/half-ten, and then we both wobble off to bed. It seemed to make a difference. It didn't knock me out, it just relaxed me more than anything. Rather than lying awake for ages I nodded off, which was absolutely fantastic.

When I woke up on the Tuesday morning I was feeling a lot better. However, it was my anniversary, the day I'd met Heidi, so it was a day of very, very mixed emotions. I was very emotional all day, thinking what it could have been like if I hadn't been in here. My poor wife, she must be thinking exactly the same thing. It was a horrible, horrible day. To top it all, I heard the guards running up the stairs and they turned the cell over again, so it was a case of putting it all back together after they left, which made the day go a little faster. Apparently, the word was that they were looking for a mobile phone. God knows how we're going to get one of those in there! They really searched hard for it, but there was no phone otherwise we would have been using it! Apparently, if you're caught with a mobile phone it's another two years on your sentence, so there's definitely an incentive not to have a mobile phone.

After lunch, I start having a granny nap for about an hour. About one-ish I go back to bed and try and sleep a bit, mainly just to make the time go faster because it's just so tedious. There's nothing going on. I've read every magazine, everything I can that's in English, really just to let the time go.

That evening I did my first canteen order. You get a little requisite paper and you write on there the bits and pieces you need. It transpired that Billy's got no money, there's a problem with his money, so he feels really embarrassed because he's a guy that doesn't want to take, take, take. He's a genuine kind of bloke. I said to Billy if you need stuff, I'll get it for you. I got Billy's cigarettes and shampoo and bits and pieces that he needed – deodorant, toilet paper, of course, all those things, and Billy likes the tea bags, so I got him some tea. You put your requisite papers in the little plastic box on the door for the following morning and when they come up for Syem at eight o'clock, they take them all down. That night I saw the little owl on the window sill again, which was nice, especially because it was my anniversary. It felt like a little message from home. It was lovely.

Wednesday

Not much goes on in the morning. Same old routine but I as turn the kettle on for my morning coffee there is this god-awful smell. The kettle has the remains of last night's dinner in it. So, I wash it out with normal tap water, several times and then let it boil a couple of times before filling it with my bottled water. Fifteen minutes later I have my coffee. It becomes apparent that Medi cooks up any scraps from peoples' plates and has a midnight snack! Normally he cleans the kettle out but this time he had forgotten.

The canteen arrives at about half past three in the afternoon. I get my forty cigarettes, a tube of toothpaste, a phone card, some new shampoo, because by now my eyes are really sore. I've bought Pantene now, so we're going to give that a go! Hopefully it's a little bit better than the last one! Of course, I get my coffee as well. Billy gets all his stuff, so he's really happy. Generally, when the canteen comes up people become a little bit more relaxed. There's less rowing, less fighting, because people are content, they've got a few bits and pieces. Cigarettes are the main problem, but they all seem to get their cigarettes on a Wednesday and are quite calm.

Thursday

Always looking forward to a Thursday because it's phone call day. We go downstairs at nine o'clock, the usual guys. The phone call goes straight through. I'm dead excited. Heidi's there. She's got the whole gang there, in fact. Zoe, my daughter, is there, the boys are there, really excited. The big news is that Heidi's found a lawyer – London Legal International up in town, recommended to her by I believe the British government, but I'm not sure. They've got an office in Turkey and an office in London. Heidi said they're not cheap, but they've said they can help you. I'm dead excited about this and Heidi says the lawyer should be coming to the prison soon to see me. So, there's a sense of relief that things are happening behind the scenes.

Then Heidi tells me: "By the way, Toby, you're front page of The Sun! You're bigger than Miley Cyrus! Miley Cyrus has only got a little bit on the side of the front page and you cover the rest!" Oh my word! It's hard to understand, it really is, having never been front page of anything before. The British people are interested in what's going on with me and about my case. I've been nicknamed

"Coin Dad" or something! It's absolutely amazing news and I love that the British people give a damn. Huge sense of relief. Before, I think I felt I was a little bit forgotten and because I'm just a normal guy, nobody gives a damn about who you are and why you're there, so to have all this information that people cared was a huge boost. I was bouncing off the walls when I went upstairs, absolutely buzzing.

Friday

More rowing, more constant fighting. Everybody's getting on my nerves, all except Billy, I guess. I was called down to get my prison ID and guess what? They had still spelled my name wrong Jonh, but hey ho! I've got my prison ID and I'm supposed to carry that at all times when I'm outside the cell. People are really getting on my nerves now. They come at you with flip flops and it's got to a point now where I don't try and talk my way out of it, I just punch them because it seems to be the only way to get anything through to them. It just carries on, it's crazy.

Saturday

I remember I went down to the Barsha for the last time for about an hour. I gave it another shot, purely just to get out of the cell, a change of scenery, but it was hotter than Hell. It was the same old thing and after an hour I was glad to get back up to the cell and shower.

Monday

On the news there's big talk about foreign national prisoners being deported back to their own countries. There's a huge sense of hope and relief within the cell. All these guys that had been there and have got huge sentences all have a little bit of hope that they might be able to get deported back to their own countries. I think some were a little bit worried because their sentences might get increased rather than decreased, but certainly the Syrian nationals – because Turkey's at war with Syria, they believe that their sentence will be quashed straight away, and they'll be released back into society. Everybody's talking about it, even between the landings. The Daesh terrorist lads, the Feto lads, they're all talking about it. Ali's French-Belgian, so he's excited too. He's talking about going home. Big, big talk.

There's also a politician called Kamal, who I think is the leader of the opposition, and he started marching around Turkey and he's got this huge following of people, supporters, that march with him. He's basically marching to raise awareness for the conditions in prisons, the foreign nationals in prisons, the fact that they're so overcrowded, and how these prisoners should be released back to their own countries. Let their own countries sort out these people's problems, rather than leaving it all in Turkey and Turkey footing the bill for it all. Plus, he's saying that the foreign nationals should be released almost immediately, or at least within a few months. This is big, big news, It seems as though the president of Turkey is starting to listen – well he can't help but listen when there's all these thousands and thousands of people marching through Turkey. Big news, a bit of excitement.

Tuesday 5th
All the courts return from their holiday, so we're hoping that things might start to get rolling again. A lot of people have been

waiting for their sentencing, for their courts, for their appeals, but the courts have had a month's holiday, so now hopefully things will start moving again. The big news is nine hundred and fifty judges throughout Turkey have been sacked. I don't know why, for what reason, but there's some new judges being appointed. I think the sentencing is perhaps too extreme, too high, people are getting a stupid amount of years where it would be better to give them a smaller time to reduce the overcrowding in prisons, that's my guess.

About half past four in the afternoon, I get called down. "Mr Toby, your lawyer's here." Whoa! My lawyer! Fantastic! Very, very excited. The usual you've got to put long trousers on, I don't have any, explain, explain, explain. Down we go, walking through the corridor to a place I've never been before. At the gates at the end, where I came in the first time, there was a little turning to the left and a small corridor. I remember the stench of this paint. It was so strong, like out of the nineteen thirties when there was all sorts of nasties in paint! It took your breath away. It gave you a headache it was so strong. We walked down this little corridor and on the right-hand side there are lots of windows – there must be about ten windows – with a bench on one side and a bench on the other, with a phone on the wall. I thought my lawyer will be on the other side of one of these, but no. There was a big iron gate at the end. I waited there for maybe ten minutes with a few other Turkish prisoners.

They didn't say anything to me – there was just a nod, an acknowledgement – and then the door opened and my name was called. In I went. This chap dressed in a white shirt, clean-shaven, smiling – the sort of bloke you instantly like – didn't really remind me of a lawyer with his stuffed shirt and his business suit, he just seemed like a normal kind of guy. He had his suit jacket hanging on the back of the chair, he just seemed approachable. He introduced himself as Murat Yilmaz. He was a lovely guy – great meeting, loads of information. Every question I asked him he had an answer for, so it was very, very refreshing in that I'd been asking lots of questions in prison and had got no answers at all, or only assumptions from other prisoners, so nothing definite, whereas here I'm talking to a lawyer who says right this will happen, this won't happen and so on. It was so, so refreshing. Really, really nice guy and great English too.

At the end of the meeting he gave me his card and asked me if I needed some money put into my canteen. I wasn't sure how much I had left, so I said yes please and on his way out he put some money into my account (£50, or the Turkish equivalent) and that was that. I was then escorted back up to the cell.

Everybody crowded round – they wanted to know about my lawyer. In particular, they wanted to know where he was from. When I said he was from Izmir they were all very impressed. Lawyers from Izmir – it's a big court – and they said he's going to be good, he deals with big cases, very big cases, so he's going to be a great lawyer. A lot of them asked to see the card and I could see people writing down his name, phone number and address off his card. I remember chatting it through with Billy. I was very excited and very positive. I could see Billy was obviously really happy for me, but it was becoming apparent that he was worried that his lawyer wasn't as good as mine. He couldn't even have a conversation without a translator with his lawyer, whereas mine had perfect English. So I think Billy was happy, but slightly miffed and depressed that his wasn't as great as mine. All good for me, but a little bit worried about Billy.

Wednesday

I bought Billy's canteen yet again – he's still out of money. We don't know what's going on with his money. He's been asking his wife for money and she says she's sent it, but it's just not getting through. Billy's really, really embarrassed about his money. He's had to borrow from a couple of the other prisoners – a couple of the paedophile French lads up the end, so he owes them money. He owes me money, but of course I wouldn't take his money anyway. I tell him not to worry, Murat's put money into my account so whatever he needs I'll get for him, just don't worry. I've always got Billy's back and I'm sure he's got mine.

Thursday

Dead excited! Always excited about Thursdays. You get to speak to your family. I've got some messages from Billy to Charlene (Billy's wife) and then I give messages to Heidi about Billy, so that if we do have a problem with the phone lines then at least one of us can get the messages through. Heidi and Charlene are talking and of course they're helping each other through what needs to be done in the UK, the best way to go about things, getting money to us, getting clothes to us. I think it's a great thing for Heidi and a great thing for Charlene that they've got something in common and both of their husbands are in the same cell together, which is great – well not great for us obviously being there, but great for them.

There's more talk from Heidi about the press. I've been in all the papers. She says everything that the press have said so far is positive. There's a sense of disbelief that this could have gone this far. They're still reporting that I'm missing – I think it was The Mirror or The Mail, I can't remember, saying that Toby's in Turkey, he's being held, but no one knows where he is. Some of the other papers are saying that I'm in Milas prison and of course I'm not!

I'm in Mugla. I'm really flattered, and shocked really in some ways that I'm still in the papers and that it's still massive in the UK. Heidi tells me that she's been talking to Tim Loughton, our MP. He's been round to see her, he's extremely supportive and he's done his bit by getting Boris Johnson and the Foreign Office involved and they're doing all they can. We talk about Murat, the new lawyer, how good he was. She was worried that he might not be up to scratch, but he definitely is. I explain that I'm really pleased with him, really excited. The whole gang's there again – Zoe's there, lots of questions, a bit of emotion obviously. I always try and talk to Brody, but he just won't say anything to me which is heart-breaking for me, but I completely understand. He says he just likes to hear Daddy's voice. Baxter, however, he waffles away – "Love you, Dad. Love you, Dad." Billy only gets three minutes of phone call, so it was really lucky that I had some messages for Heidi to give to Charlene.

Later on, up in the cell during the afternoon Billy's really worried and he starts quizzing me about my lawyer. I explain I'm going to write my statement and I ask Billy, "Do you want me to write your statement for you?" Billy just lights up. He says, "Tobe, that would be great! I write like a spider and my spelling's not great and I'm really quite embarrassed about it." I said, "Billy, don't worry, mate! You tell me your story and I'll write it all down for you." Five pages later I've heard this unbelievable story, absolutely unbelievable.

The gist of it is that Billy got drugged or his drink was spiked in a club or bar in Marmaris. He was with a family friend. He and she left the bar purely and simply because they started blacking out and feeling really weird. It sounds to me like Rohypnol, but I don't know. They left the bar and wandered down to the port area where all the boats are moored. Some huge boats down there. They were looking for somewhere, a bit of refuge where they could just sit down and chill out and get their thoughts together, get some fresh air. As they walked past one of the boats the canopy was open on the back, so they nipped in there and sat down quietly for a bit.

Eventually, Billy's friend she got off – Billy was fumbling around trying to turn a TV on on the back of the boat. He still doesn't know why – obviously the drugs that he had taken were messing him up. He finally gave up, walked off the boat and his friend had disappeared. He spent ages looking for her. Eventually, he got in the car, assuming she must have gone back to the villa in a taxi and shot back there.

A few hours later the phone rings and Billy's friend is saying, "Billy, you've got to come back! This boat we were on, it's on fire!" Billy said, "Look, I can't drive, I'm absolutely a mess." So, the police come and pick him up and with that Billy is arrested for murder. Billy's saying, "What are you talking about? I don't know what you're talking about!" It transpires that the boat caught fire and the fire spread to the two neighbouring boats and unfortunately on one of the boats there were two guys asleep. One perished in the fire and the other one was extremely badly burnt. Both Billy and his friend were arrested and that was back on April 11th 2017. That's a brief version of Billy's story: arrested and thrown into Mugla.

Me and Heidi, happier times!!!

Me and the boys, dinner out.

Rented a Jet ski.

Fun in the pool, my shoulders though!!

Birthday card to Baxter, Billy slipped to Charlene on his visit!!

Outside the hospital after yet another medical on 02/10/17 with Murat. Finally going home. Flip flops held together with string and two stone lighter!!

Murat sent this to Heidi. Me saying goodbye to Murat, unintentionally setting the alarms off at Dalman airport while airport security are closing in.

Reunited at last, Gatwick airport 02/10/17

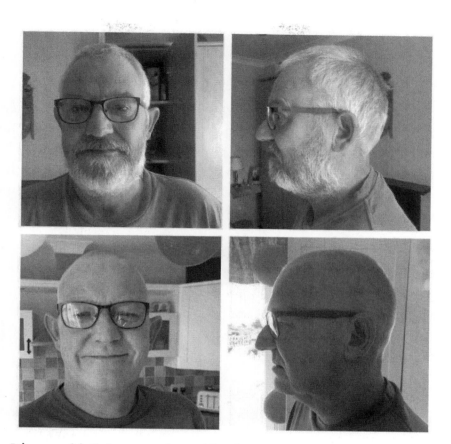

It's my birthday, getting rid of the fuzz, haircut and shave
03/10/17

Chapter Five

<u>Friday 8th September</u>

A new cell mate arrives, a guy called Felshat from Azerbaijan. First thing that strikes me about him is he's a big guy, he's probably eighteen/nineteen stone, quite young – probably late twenties. He's wearing this enormous blue T-shirt and he's carrying about this red rag, which apparently is a sweat cloth; they use it to wipe the sweat off when it's hot.

Every time I look at him all I think of Iggle Piggle! The character from the kids' TV show. I can't help but almost liking him, but then he seems to act like Iggle Piggle as well! It just catches me comical. It's the stupid things that amuse you when you're under these extreme situations, but Iggle Piggle's arrived! He moves in beside me, in Vlad's old bed.

He eats as much as he can. He's a big lad, so he devours the contents of the fridge, not that there's ever much in there, but he goes through it. If he's not eating he's sleeping. He lays there on his bed with his shorts on, takes his blue T-shirt off, wraps it round his eyes to keep the light out and puts this little red handkerchief thing over his big fat belly and that's him done. He just goes to sleep. Very amusing character. He's already annoyed lots of people by raiding the fridge and nicking everybody's water, in particular mine, he keeps nicking my water. He keeps nicking my cigarettes. I've already said to him, if you want a cigarette, please help yourself, but just ask! That's all I want, just can I take a cigarette, can I take some water. I'm never going to deprive anybody of water! I've got plenty of water under my bed in big five litre containers, so please help yourself! I'm happy to share, but just ask.

Saturday

The weekend's coming now, it's Saturday. It's one of those things that nobody looks forward to – it's so quiet, so depressing, nothing goes on, nothing changes. The usual rows, the usual fights. Horrible, horrible. Hate the weekends! Iggle Piggle is still finding his feet. He's big enough so people don't push him around, but people are not happy with him at all.

Sunday

Really early Sunday morning, must have been about two in the morning, I heard something under my bed and there was Iggle Piggle leaning out of his bed – the beds were very, very close, all cramped into a small space – Iggle Piggle with his hand under my bed helping himself to my cigarettes. In the way I was lying on the bed I managed this well-aimed slap and it was a proper crack, right across his cheek! The shock on his face was unbelievable, bless him. He didn't know what to do. I said to him in English, "If you want a cigarette, you ask." With that I got up, I gave him the cigarette, had one for myself, we lit them both and we sat there in silence. I was thinking hopefully you'll understand that I'm just a normal bloke, and all you have to do is ask and I'll give you a cigarette.

That Sunday everybody was running out of cigarettes. There were only a few of us that had them and I didn't have many because people had been nicking them, I'd been bribing the guards for this, that and other, I'd got letters written earlier on in the week before I'd done the templates, so I was running out too. However it was still easier to give my cigarettes away to keep the peace. Everybody was rowing, everybody.

Monday

Monday was hard. Although it was Monday and things were starting to happen for me, good things, I kept thinking it's still a long way away before I get to court, so I was getting a bit depressed, I guess. I start switching off almost, trying to block my family out, because every time I think about my family, my friends, my work colleagues, it hurts. I start to get really emotional, upset, so I'm trying really hard now to block it out. I start to just concentrate more on the prisoners and the cell and the boring, ball-aching routines that we have to put up with every day, so really trying hard to block everything out. However, a little bit later on, we end up with another new cell mate.

This guy's called Hamed and he's from Iran. He comes in and we're all asking him what have you been up to and why are you here. He said it was just a problem with his paperwork. He slots in beside me, by the foot end of the bed, so now there's four in a tiny little space. We've got Medi, me, Iggle Piggle and now we've got Hamed, who's very well-preened, likes to talk about himself and is very confident and cocksure; he comes across as a little bit arrogant. He started off with this story about his paperwork not being in order. We just brushed it under the carpet.

Then Iggle Piggle comes up the cell. We're all sitting by the TV – Iggle Piggle walks up and we ask him his story. Nobody's really had a conversation with him yet, because all he does it eat and sleep. It transpires that Iggle Piggle was caught smuggling refugees. He picked them up in Syria and was taking them to Greece and had been intercepted by the Turkish coastguard. He had thirty refugees on board at a price of US$5,000 – each. A huge amount of money.

He'd been caught and that was that. However, watching the television, nine times out of ten everybody gets reported on at some point, all the prisoners.

Whilst we were sitting there watching CNN Turk a video came up of this huge inflatable boat cram-packed full of refugees. There was a little chap on the back with quite a big outboard being hunted down by the Turkish coastguard. We watched the coastguard put a rope in the water with a buoy attached to the other end of it, so it was a floating rope, and they drove in front of the inflatable boat and as the rope went underneath the boat, it just ripped the outboard completely off the back of the boat. The cameras all zoom in and guess whose face we see? Hamed! The Iranian! So we're all looking at him saying, "Problem with your paperwork? I don't think so! You were smuggling refugees! Maybe you should change your bullshit story?" He came clean in the end. He had sixty one or sixty two refugees in this boat at US$5,000 a hit, going from Syria to Greece, when he was intercepted when the coastguard ripped his engine off the back, which is now somewhere at the bottom of the Mediterranean! So his bullshit story didn't stick around for too long! He speaks a little bit of Turkish, so perhaps we can use his skills (if we trust him!) for a bit of chat with the guards and maybe getting a few more things done; taking him down when you go down to see the warden as a translator maybe.

That night I remember seeing the little owl again. Always have a tear in my eye when a little owl appears on the window sill. Always brings me a sense of comfort. It's probably me being daft, but it's just nice to know that your wife is there beside you. It's lovely.

Tuesday 12th

Hamed is really struggling. He's only been in here less than twenty four hours and he's pacing up and down the cell for hours and hours. We're only talking about fifteen/twenty metres up and down the cell. It's up, turn around. Down, turn around. Up, turn around, and so on. It goes on forever. Later on we find out that he was in this exact prison, this exact cell, two years ago. We never found out what he'd done previously, but I would imagine it was the same sort of thing – smuggling refugees.

Iggle Piggle keeps stealing my water! Yet again! So by now I'm getting really fed up with it all. I've tried to explain to him, I've tried to be nice. My water bottle that I keep beside my pillow – which is what everybody does – I emptied it out and filled it up with the water from the bucket beside the toilet, the one they use to wash their arses in and then put it back beside my pillow on my bed and then just waited to see what's going to happen!

Seka, he finally gets his hospital appointment and off he goes. We don't see him for a couple of hours. He gets dressed – we've never really seen him in his outside clothes before. He's always wearing rags around the cell. He puts on his clothes, the same stuff he was wearing when he robbed a little old lady in a wheelchair. He strikes me as being like the Rocker from the Mods and Rockers era! That's kind of what he looked like when he went out of the cell! He comes back, really excited, really happy. He's got new medication to keep his nerves and anxiety down, to calm him basically. He's certainly in need of some new medication, because the other stuff doesn't seem to be touching the sides.

Billy's still got no money. People are trying to get cigarettes from the terrorists all day. They're throwing down bits of string and making tea for the terrorists, and for all the lads downstairs and sending it down on bottles and then they get a couple of cigarettes in return for a bottle of tea. It's really hard with the cigarette thing.

Then I get called out by the guards. "You've got a meeting with your lawyer." At which point Medi gets really excited and explains that he's coming with me. No, it's not happening, Medi! I'm going down on my own. I explain that, I will tell my lawyer that you want to see him. Write me a letter next time, I'll take it down with me and if you want to employ him as your lawyer then you can. They've all asked me to ask my lawyer when I next see him about the deportation and all the things that are going on with the government with regards to foreign nationals. They're kind of excited and want a bit of information, but I don't suppose Medi can wait. He wants to quiz him himself. I said no. Medi's not happy obviously, but he'll have to get over it. I go down to see Murat alone.

I see the ever smiling Murat and he immediately puts me at ease. He explains that we've got a meeting booked in with the judge and that's planned for the 25th, so not far away at all. I'm hugely excited. He describes this meeting to me not as court, but as a meeting. We're going to go there, we're going to explain the misunderstanding and then hopefully I'll be released. He said it is a simple misunderstanding and we should be able to iron it out with the judge, avoiding the need to go to court. Okay, fine, I'm really happy with that. Just go there and have a chat with the judge and I'm free, sounds simple. Of course, I've got this perfect translator in Murat who can tell my story. I've got my statement ready and everything, so it's perfect. I'm really, really excited and relieved.

I ask Murat, firstly about Billy. I explain to him about Billy. Murat's face says it all really. He said, "Toby, look, it's not a simple case, not like yours where you haven't done anything wrong. You were given the coins, or your children were given the coins, and you're completely innocent. It's a case where somebody's actually died and it's manslaughter. I don't want to give Billy any hope and I don't want to tell him it's really bad, but we have to be honest." I really liked this about Murat. He didn't beat about the bush – it was just black is black and white is white.

Then I asked him about the deportation and he said it had already started. In places like Ankara, Istanbul and Izmir, things have already started to move. In those prisons, in that area – I don't know what prisons they were – the wheels are in motion. Some prisoners have been given their paperwork already and have dates for deportation, so this was great news. Finally something's happening for the lads upstairs too, even though I can't stand most of them and I row with them all day long. Some of them haven't spoken to their families in two years, so the chance of getting out of the hell-hole that we're in is great for them. Nobody deserves to be in a place like this.

Murat also mentions that it might be possible to get me transferred to a different prison; what he described as an open prison. It's a prison just for foreigners, but you have a bit more freedom. You actually have some sort of recreational area, so you're not confined to your cell all day long. Pretty much immediately I said we've got this meeting with the judge planned and I've got access to funds, so I can buy things, and most importantly I've got a contact with you and my family. At least I'm granted a ten minute phone call. I don't want to have to go to another prison and go through all of that rigmarole again of getting phone calls sorted out

Of course, the other reason was Billy. I was very worried about leaving Billy. He's pretty low at the moment, extremely low. He's not in a good place at all. I feel I have a bit of a responsibility towards Billy. He's got no money, he's got nothing. Then he's had a three minute phone call with Charlene on the Thursday and his life's just a bit of a mess. For those reasons I decided that I would stay and endure hopefully the short time that I was to be left in Mugla.

Back upstairs it's big news for all the cell mates when I go back. I say things are moving, things are happening! There's a general sense of excitement up there. The only one that's not really that excited is Medi. He's got the arse with me because I wouldn't let him come downstairs and he's got no cigarettes and Medi is properly doing is nut! Absolutely doing his nut! He's shouting and swearing: "I need cigarettes! I need cigarettes!" ringing the buzzer for the guards to come up. "I need cigarettes now!" We're laughing at him, you just have to get over it. You're in prison, what do you expect? The cigarettes we've got left, we all share out anyway. Billy's got a few, I've a got few. I don't smoke that much anyway, I still only have a couple of puffs every now and then. One cigarette would have done me until the canteen came. Anything to keep the peace.

Wednesday

It can't arrive soon enough! Wednesday morning is a bit of a blur, food in the kettle again. People are still rowing and fighting over cigarettes, but Wednesday afternoon the canteen arrives. I've never seen anybody open a pack of cigarettes so quickly in all my life as Medi! It was my packet actually, but he opened it up, lit a cigarette and just sat back and relaxed. He then spent the rest of the afternoon rolling cigarettes. These were called Tatun. You get a box of what look like empty cigarettes and a packet of tobacco. There should be a machine supplied but because it contains a piece of sharp metal so they are forbidden. Medi spends ages poking tobacco down into the cigarettes with an old straw. You could see the relief on this guy's face! So there's a sense of contentment throughout the whole of the Terras cell! No major rows in the afternoon. It's all pretty good.

But then later on, at about four or five o'clock, I heard this God awful noise. I walked towards the toilet area and there was Iggle Piggle, both ends – diarrhoea and vomiting. I went and had a quick look in my bed and there was half a bottle of my water missing. Obviously I hadn't gone near it. I'd been drinking out of the five litre ones under my bed. Iggle Piggle had done himself up on the water they use to wash their charlies in! Not a well bunny!

Thursday

Big day, Thursday. Phone call to the guys. Iggle Piggle's not well – he's been up pretty much all night. Before we left to go downstairs for the phone call, Iggle Piggle was in the cupboard under the stairs, the loo, I think maybe I've done him up too well. I spoke to Heidi and the boys. We were talking about the 25th. They were slightly confused. They didn't know anything at all about it, about the day I was supposed to go and see the judge, they hadn't heard, which was a little bit troubling for me because I thought they would have known before me. We were all talking about it, we're all very excited, I remember that. Just a really nice phone call. Heidi was saying that the Foreign Office had been in contact. The Turkish Ambassador in London had been calling her. The British Ambassador had been in contact with my judge, so there's an awful lot of pressure being put on the judge. There's mention now that Theresa May PM has got involved and she's been writing e-mails to Erdoğan, the President of Turkey. There's an immense sense of pride that the British Government are discussing me at cabinet meetings and are really working hard to get me out. I've never been so proud to be British in all my life. I'd been singing the National Anthem – not every day, but every other day perhaps– quite loud just to show, even though I don't pray and I don't shout, I'm very patriotic and very proud to be British. So much so that some of the lads, after the first two lines of the song, they would join in with the four la la la's followed my a huge cheer! So it all became a bit of light relief!

In the afternoon, I touched up my statement for court. It wasn't really a statement-statement, it was just a list of things that I had to remember, I had to remember to mention. Bullet points really to remind me of what I had to include. I'm sitting around counting down the days really. Iggle Piggle's getting a little bit bullied now and I do feel a bit sorry for him after not making him drink the toilet water, but leaving it around for him to find. I do feel a little bit guilty, because he's not well at all. I start warming a bit to him – not a great deal, because he's still very ignorant and thieving git.

In the evening, Seka's got a problem with his medication. They bring all our tablets up at about half past seven every night, which is about half an hour before Syem. They brought mine and Billy's up, but they didn't bring his. I've stopped taking my sleeping tablets now. I've been giving them to other lads. I'm not a big fan of taking tablets. They've got me back into a better sleep pattern though. If I'm dead tired and I can't sleep then I will take one, but generally I give them to Billy. If I leave then he might not get any more and I was worried. It was me that got him the doctor's appointment and he might not be able to get another one, so at least he'd have a few weeks' worth. Generally I give them to Billy, but also to some of the other lads too.

Seka, bless him, he's not got his medication at half-seven. When they come up for Syem, Seka asked for his medication. "Yeah, we'll bring it up later," he gets told. "Bekra, bekra," which means "later". Nine o'clock he rings the bell on the outside of the cell. He's starting to panic now. They come up, no medication. He asks and they keep telling him later, later. He's walking around the cell, he's pulling his hair out, he doesn't know what to do with himself. About ten o'clock he rings the bell one more time.

They come up and he goes for them through the cell door. He starts shouting at them. They walk in and I grabbed hold of Seka and calmed him down, tried to get in between him and the two guards, because it looked like he was going to go for the guards and that's never a good move. I stood between them and kept them apart, but he was shouting and swearing at them in Arabic. They disappeared and I thought it was all over. A couple of minutes later, about ten/twelve of them came back, took him outside the cell and on the landing just outside the cell. Two of them held his arms and the other eight or ten just punched the living daylights out of him. Then they threw him down the stairs. We were all watching this, or the ones crowding round the gate were, all shouting at the guards to leave him alone. They took him off and probably at about half past eleven he came back. Bruises and cuts – he looked like hell.

They finally gave him his medication and he spent the rest of the night crying himself to sleep. We tried to help him out. I sat on his bed for a while, but he was pretty much inconsolable. I did feel sorry for him.

<u>Friday morning</u>

I wake up, Seka's asleep. We were all a bit worried he might try and kill himself again, but he didn't. I remember putting my fingers on the side of his neck, checking his pulse, making sure he was alive, but he was out for the count with a good strong pulse, bless him, sleeping off the night before's saga. Billy gets a letter at syem and after translation tells me that he's going to get a meeting today. His wife Charlene is coming to see him. I said would it be okay if I drew a little birthday card that he could smuggle to Charlene. Billy agrees without hesitation. I quickly write a little birthday card and draw a cartoon with a little character that I call Oswald – this poor little fella sitting behind bars in Mugla M1-11! I say: *I'm really sorry that I can't be with you today, but hope I'll see you soon. Lots of love, Dad.* I give that to Billy and off he goes.

He's supposed to have an hour with Charlene, but after about forty five minutes he comes back upstairs. He's happy he's seen Charlene, but he's not in the best of moods because the guards cut his visit short. It's cost Charlene a thousand pounds to come over with flights, hotel, taxis, etc. It costs a thousand pounds every time she comes over and she gets forty minutes with Billy, which is ridiculous. Billy's not best pleased, but at least they got to see each other and have a kiss and a cuddle. However, it's all supervised, they're not left to their own devices. He says he's given Charlene Baxter's card. So it's all good news.

Later that afternoon the guards appear at the gate and summon the Captain. They give him a plastic box, about the size of a small shoe box. The Captain goes and sits on his bed and I don't think any more of it. Over the next half hour or so I keep glancing over at him, lots of head scratching going on. Eventually he comes over and hands be the box. I open the lid and inside is a diabetes kit, containing insulin, syringes, needles and a BM kit to test his sugar levels, however there were no instructions or prescriptions. I like the Captain and I want to help him but this is way above my pay grade. I know that if you take too much insulin it's game over so I'm going to have to be really careful. I can't believe that these idiots have not included a prescription. I remember feeling a huge sense of responsibility and anger towards the prison system, how bloody ridiculous. I started by taking his BM and then slowly injecting very small amounts of insulin morning and evening over the first week until his BM stabilised at around 12. For the first three days at least I gave him the jabs because he was frightened to death and then slowly but surely he started sorting himself out. They hadn't even told him to keep the insulin in the fridge.

Normal Friday really: shower in the afternoon, which was lovely except for the rows, fights, and the same old rubbish that came with it. At about half past seven we all get a call from the guards to come up to the gate. It's haircut time. For 10 TL you get to have your hair cut. This is great news, I'm going to look half decent for court. Everyone files through the gate onto the landing and off we go. However the guards single me out and tell me to wait behind. They say that my lawyer's here. I'm thinking this can't be right. Something fishy is going on. It's half past seven, my lawyer wouldn't be here. He's from Izmir – that's three hours' drive away – something's up. I remember taking my watch off, taking my glasses off and leaving them in the cell, thinking something's up, I'm going to get a beating or something's wrong. So I walk downstairs and they usher me through to where I'd been before to see my lawyer. I still don't know what's going on.

My name's called, through the gate I go and there he is! Murat! "What are you doing here? It's half past seven!" He explains that they were releasing eighteen prisoners, so he had to wait. He'd waited in the car outside for three hours to see me! I was gob smacked and also seriously impressed that this lawyer had spent three hours waiting to see his client. Seriously impressed with Murat. My confidence is obviously growing.

I spoke to him about Billy again – gave him Billy's statement – and then we went through my statement. I said to Murat can you give me some coaching? What do I need to say? He said: "Toby, you've done nothing wrong. You're an innocent man, so the easiest thing is just to tell the truth. It is the truth, so say the truth." This gave me an immense sense of relief, because I'm not one for trying to embellish or change stories to suit courts or somebody else. If I can just stand there and rattle off exactly what happened, it's dead easy. That was a huge relief. I was really worried about that. He said: "You must remember to mention four things, but they're all true too, so you don't have to worry." I said, "What are the four things?" He said, "The first thing is that you went there on holiday – a family holiday with your wife and the boys, a two week holiday, in Turkey and that's all it was. No other reason you went to Turkey." Okay, fine, that's the truth. The second thing I had to mention was that I didn't know it was a crime to collect the coins, so that's also true. The third thing was that I didn't know it was a crime to take historical coins or artefacts from Turkey, which I hadn't tried to do in retrospect because I'd declared them at Customs. However, I stuck with that one. The fourth was that I had a family at home in England that depended on me and my salary to get by. All of these four things were things I probably would have said anyway. So an immense sense of relief in that I didn't have to try and change my story or make it fit somebody else's needs. It was just tell the truth. Great news. No hair cut but so what; the other lads are all sporting number two crew cuts though.

Chapter Six

<u>Saturday 16th</u>

We're half-way through September now and I can't wait for this month to fly by. I keep singing Green Day, *Wake Me Up When September Ends* over and over in my head. It's like my most depressing song. It's a great song, but it's very apt at the moment. However, Billy's feeling a bit more positive now; after I'd done his statement he's feeling a whole lot better, more confident. Iggle Piggle – he's sorted himself out a bit. He's coming round a little bit more, he's even engaging in conversation. He's coming out of his shell. Hamed – he's becoming more likeable. Once he got caught out with the lies and rubbish he was talking about with his paperwork, he's accepting people a bit more now. Medi approaches me with a brand spanking new tracksuit that one of the French paedophile's dad's had given him. He said, "Toby, you can wear this for court." I think they're all a bit worried that I'm going to turn up in court with shorts and a T-shirt that are prison-worn, to say the least. They're all rummaging around trying to help me out.

So Medi has given me this tracksuit and a brand spanking new pair of trainers, albeit they're a size eight and I'm a size ten, they are at least brand spanking new and very wearable, just a little bit small and pinching my toes! I think I'll have to get over it! The tracksuit though – I can't help feeling that I look like some sort of football hoodie! So I'm a little bit anxious and worried about wearing that!

Sunday 17th, morning

Baxter's birthday, dead excited. I am going to get to speak to Baxter and wish him a happy birthday. Basically I'm going get two phone calls in a week, so I feel like I've won the lottery! Got one over on the prison system! I can't wait to speak to Baxter. As soon as the guards come up for Syem at eight o'clock, I say, "Phone call, phone call, what about my phone call?!" I'm all over them. They say, "Bekra, bekra," which means "later". You hear that quite a lot in prison. It's either "bekra" which means "later", "tomorrow" is "yarin", or "yok" which just means "no". They pretty much all mean the same thing. I've booked the phone call, I know it's going to happen and I'm dead excited about it. They come up at about nine for something else and I ask them again. I say, "Look lads, telephone, telephone!" I even show them the bit of paper that I've got from the warden or manager number two. They say bekra, bekra, bekra. I say, "What time?" and they say ten o'clock. So ten o'clock comes, it goes, and I push the bell on the outside. A couple of guards come up and I say about the telephone, show them the paperwork. I'm getting a bit frustrated now obviously. I said to them, you said ten and it's now half-ten and why haven't I got the phone call? Eleven o'clock comes and goes, then they bring the lunch up at twelve (rice and beans time), so I ask them again, "Can I have the telephone?" They say when lunch is finished. I wait 'til one o'clock. They come back up and the trustee takes away all the tea urns that the food comes up in. This time the gate's open, so I walk out and I confront these two guards. I said, "You've told me all morning, from eight o'clock this morning and it's now one o'clock. Why have I got no phone call?" They say no. No phone call, yok, it's not happening, no phone call, it's finished. They wipe their hands, which basically means it's not happening, it's finished, that's the end of the conversation.

At this point I get very, very angry. I start shouting at the guards telling them exactly what I think of them. They march me back into the cell. Ten minutes later, not even that probably, they come back up, ask for me, and I think oh fantastic! Phone call! They take me downstairs, put me in the Barsha room. I'm thinking here we go! Glasses off, watch off, windmill time. In they all come – ten/twelve guards – the usual scenario. I whip my T-shirt off and I'm thinking here we go, let's play! By then I just don't care. I'm so frustrated, so angry that these bastards have messed with me yet again and I'm not going to be able to speak to my boy, to Baxter, and wish him a happy birthday. I'm just about to let fly at all of these guys and Mahmood comes in, marches all of them out and then spends the next ten/fifteen minutes calming me down. He said, "Look, there's no way you can have your phone call now because it's too late." There was no other explanation really. He said it's not possible on a Sunday. I showed him the paperwork, the letter that I had, and he said it doesn't matter. This is all in pigeon English. He calms me down yet again and then back I go up to the cell. Pretty miserable all day long. However, the highlight was the little owl came to see me. At least I got my birthday card out with Billy, so hopefully Baxter got that, but I had no way of knowing, it's so bloody frustrating.

Monday morning

Hamed comes up to me and he says, "Look, I have jeans for your court". I'm thinking great! At least I can look half-decent! I try the jeans on and they fit absolutely perfectly. So now I've got a pair of trainers and a pair of jeans. I diplomatically, very diplomatically, give Medi back his tracksuit. Medi uses his noodle and thinks well, he's got jeans, he's got trainers, and produces this yellow cashmere jumper, also brand new. It was my size, not his size – he's very round, to say the least! No way on God's green earth would he have got it on! I gratefully accept it. I'm feeling pretty good now. My confidence has got a bit better because now I'm going to be able to look half-decent for court. I'm not going to turn up looking like some sort of beach bum. No real grumbles.

<u>Tuesday morning</u>

I woke up at about half past two. Really weird noise – it sounded like children crying. I was trying to figure out where it was coming from. I ended up getting out of bed, walking up the cell, only to find that it was coming from the gate/the main cell door. I was still trying to figure out this weird sound. As I looked through the gate, there were a few other lads getting out of bed too, it turns out to be a cat of all things! A couple of the French lads have also heard it and they walk up the cell to the gate and try to entice the cat by throwing bits of chicken through the cell door. The cat's gratefully eating this chicken! Finally, one of them, Belkas, picks up the cat and pulls it into the cell. This cat is seriously wild and very unfriendly. He bites Belkas on the thumb and then scratches the hell out of him! Belkas throws the cat, which lands on Seka. Seka hadn't woken up – it would take a nuclear bomb to wake him up on his new medication – this cat landed on him and just went ballistic! Seka wakes up screaming. There's blood and teeth and Seka's getting scratched to hell. This cat finally legs it back through the cell gate and proceeds to finish off the little bits of chicken that the lads had thrown out for him.

By now Billy's up and he's saying, "What's going on?" So we tell him all about the cat. He looks out the door and sees these bits of chicken that the cat's eating. He's wondering about where the hell this chicken's come from, because we haven't seen chicken in our food. Billy's crying out for protein – he's still working out with his water bottles. He could really do with some chicken, well we all could! Billy says, "Where's the chicken coming from?!" getting very excited but, everybody goes back to bed and it's all quiet. Later on at about seven or so we wake up. Billy can't let the chicken thing go, so he starts quizzing people.

This is all before I've had a cup of coffee. Loads of arguments all day long about this bloomin' chicken. Finally, it transpires that Medi has been stealing all the meat and giving it to the French lads. We haven't seen it, because Medi takes the pots from the door and then dishes it up in the kitchen. Secretly he's been scooping out the meat, keeping it and then giving it to the four French lads in return for six hundred cigarettes a week. We've all been wondering how Medi gets as many cigarettes as he does when he's got no money coming in. Billy's goes absolutely ballistic, so I have to calm him down and basically sit on him! Otherwise Billy's going to get caught by the guards and he'll end up down in the solitary cells, so I have to calm him down.

Billy starts dishing out the food now, so he starts taking the food from the cell door, going to the kitchen and then dishing it up. All of a sudden we start getting a little bit more food and little bits of meat. We even get five goat balls instead of three! Hip, hip, hooray!

About half-past ten that night, we have a new cell mate arrive – a guy called Marcel, who originates from Frankfurt. He's been living in Bodrum, but he's a drug dealer. He got caught with ten wraps of cocaine, two hundred and fifty grams of hashish, a set of scales, and several burner phones. Immediately, the first thing I say, no offence to Marcel, but down by me there's not enough room, so you guys will have to make some space because I'm already sleeping on top of everybody else as it is. I put up a proper resistance and say it's not happening. He needs to go down the other end of the cell where there is space, albeit occupied by your prayer mats. You will have to condense your space a little bit, pray in the smaller space and let this guy sleep there. So he slots in by the Captain in the prayer area. He's very jumpy – obviously high as a kite – and really quite annoying. I wouldn't say Germanic, but he's very confident and full of himself. He's up all night, because of course they give him nothing for drug addiction – there's no pills or medication to help him get down off of the cocaine addiction that he's got, so he's cold turkey in Turkey. Sorry!! Diarrhoea, vomiting, all night long – a proper treat for us all.

The French, they had kept me awake, chatting all night. They'd slept all day again. There's only this small sheet that cordons off their area from my bed and you can hear everything they say, everything echoes. I get out of bed eventually and go in and say, "Look guys, you've gotta shut up, otherwise the next time I come in I'm going to start slapping people!" They understand what I mean. I'm pretty grouchy because I've had no sleep and I am not in a good mood. Finally, it goes quiet and I get off to sleep.

<u>Wednesday morning</u>

Billy's still got no money, he's still feeling really embarrassed. He doesn't know what's happened to his money. Charlene keeps saying she's putting the money in. His lawyer is getting the money from Charlene and his lawyer is sending the money, so it's going missing somewhere between the lawyer and the prison. He's told everybody that there's going to be an investigation. The people he's borrowed the money from (obviously except me because I know

Billy and he's cool) they're all disbelieving him and thinking yeah, yeah, he's just full of hot air. Marcel sleeps all day. We put his food away so that if and when he does wake up he's got something to eat. We're trying to look after him, but he is what he is

Billy as I said has taken over the kitchen, so we're still getting more food. It's nowhere near enough, but it's a lot better than it was. There's still the same amount of rice, it was just the proteins that were being stolen, so now we're getting a touch more meat. It's causing a lot of rows though, because Medi is now without cigarettes because the French have said if you're not giving us the meat, we're not buying you cigarettes. So Medi's doing his nut. He's got cigarettes now, but on Wednesday when the canteen is delivered Medi's going to be without cigarettes, so we're all going to pay for that one!

The French lads were provoking me all day, because I'd been in and had a word with them in the night. They just push my buttons all day – you look tired, didn't you sleep last night and this sort of thing. In the end, I cornered the French lads, all four of them, and I said, "Look lads, this has to stop. Midnight, you turn off everything and you shut up, because I cannot deal with it. If it happens again there's going to be a whole world of pain". It's the only language they understand. It's not like me at all, but unless you physically threaten people they don't seem to get it. One of them, Fisan, he tells me it's impossible to be quiet. I argue with him, saying, "It's not impossible, it's respect". He turns around to me and he says, "I've been here longer than you, therefore I have the right to make noise." What a stupid argument! Really? You sound like a child in a playground. He gets in my face and starts threatening me, so that's it. I pin him on the bed, put my hand round his throat and I just say, "Seriously. One word after midnight, then I'm coming in and you will know I've been there". Conversation over!!

It's been a week now since the Captain started on insulin and the results are really promising. I've been keeping a diary all week of his sugar levels and he's looking much better. The swelling and redness in his legs have reduced dramatically, I must be doing something right! He's even injecting himself in a horse shoe pattern, right thigh, stomach and then left thigh. I'm feeling extremely relieved but still really disgusted at the prison. What would have happened if I hadn't been there to help him, not that I've had any experience of handing out diabetic prescriptions, that's way above my pay grade.

That evening I go to bed quite late – the film finishes about half past ten, but I hang around until about half eleven, so that I'm absolutely on my charley tired. I even break off a couple of cigarette filters and push them into my ears. They go to bed about half eleven/quarter to twelve. Low and behold, come midnight, I'm thinking oh my God! What's going to happen? Am I going to have to get all roughy-toughy? But low and behold, twelve o'clock, the place was silent, absolutely silent. There was the usual stuff from the guys downstairs, but I'd learned to accept that. The French lads were dead quiet, so it was a real breath of fresh air. In fact, on the Wednesday night, I got a pretty good night's sleep, to be fair. The cigarette filters in the ears were an absolute stroke of genius! Genius level five! For the duration of my stay there I slept with the filters in my ears. Although they were slightly uncomfortable when you turn over, it was better than hearing the noise. I slept a lot better. In fact, some of the other lads had seen what I'd done and they started doing exactly the same, so a lot of the lads started copying me and putting the filters in their ears!

Thursday morning

I wake up around seven and as I'm walking to my locker to get my coffee I glance into the shower; there's blood everywhere. After a cartoon like double take I see Iggle Piggle with a razor blade, eighteen slashes to his forearm. I shout for Billy and the others and then start shouting at Iggle Piggle to drop the blade. I forcefully sit him on his arse and he drops the blade. Blood is pumping out of him. I grab his arm and push my thumb under his biceps, pinching off the artery. This stems the bleed. I get Billy to tear up an old sheet into strips and we start to bandage him up. By now the guards have arrived and we take Iggle Piggle down to the sick bay accompanied by Hamed as translator. I think the guards understood what I was doing with my thumb but the doctor certainly didn't. He told me to release my grip on his arm. I tried to explain through Hamed but he just didn't get it, help me god! He was taking off the temporary bed sheet bandage when I let go. The doctor now covered in blood indicated that I should reapply my thumb back on to the artery. What a twat!!! It took about forty five minutes to stop the bleeding and dress the wound with adhesive bandages. The doctor then dismissed us, no ambulance, no hospital and no stitches; you couldn't make it up!! So back to the cell we went.

All this before coffee but that crappy Nescafe never tasted so good. Marcel asks for the doctor and of course the German consul. And then it's phone call – yeah! Very excited. Love Thursday mornings, love Thursdays – it's my favourite day. I go downstairs and make the call. Heidi, Zoe and the boys are there. Heidi still knows nothing about this meeting with the judge, which is slightly worrying. I'm still very excited about the meeting with the judge though. It's great to hear the family, it's lovely to talk to them. Brody still won't talk to me, the little monkey! He says he just likes to listen to Daddy's voice, which is really nice, but it just wrenches at my heart, absolutely kills me. Baxter waffles on as usual – he talks for both of them! It's really, really nice. Really good phone call. The end is in sight now. I've got dates, things happening, so I'm counting down the days, which is really quite nice. A lot of the other lads in there of course they've got no goals, they've got nothing to talk about, nothing to look forward to. Whereas me, I know, whether it be good or bad, at least I'm going to court, at least something's happening.

On the way up I hear this massive commotion after the phone call. Wondering what the hell is going on, I get escorted up with the French lads. We get back upstairs and there's no Billy and I'm thinking what's going on here? It seems like Billy was the commotion. We wait and wait and wait. It seems that Billy has had a row with his wife Charlene. She's asked him probing questions about the girl he was with in Turkey, Rosie, and that's sent Billy over the edge. Billy's properly stressed at the moment and this has sent him over the edge. I spent the next two hours calming Billy down and sorting him out.

After the two hours, Fisan decides to wind Billy up, just get in his face and provokes him. First about food, because they're obviously not getting the amount of chicken and meat and whatever they were getting before, and then he touches on Charlene and the phone call. Well, Billy absolutely goes ballistic. He punches the lockers and the dent in these lockers was pretty impressive. Billy's absolutely fuming. You can hear the guards running up the stairs. I just sit on Billy and say, "Look, mate, just chill, chill the fuck out, because otherwise you're going to go downstairs confined to solitary." So by the time the guards get upstairs, there's me and Billy sitting on his bed – I've got a magazine and we're just chatting. The guards come in and look over wondering what's what! We just look at them perplexed and puzzled, like what do you want?! They say something in Turkish and we just said we don't understand. They throw their eyes in the air and off they go! So the guards are pacified and disappear.

Fisan's learned his lesson – he runs down the cell and basically hides from Billy, because he knows what's going to happen if he gets in Billy's way. Billy's changing, he's changing a lot. I know he's going to miss me and I think he knows I might be going home soon and then he's left with the rest of these nutters. He's got nothing in common with any of them. They all speak this weird generic Arabic, which he doesn't understand. His only cell mate is going to be Marcel, who's got some English, but he's a very, very arrogant man.

Seka goes off to prison court. This is like a "kangaroo court" within the prison itself – it's not a proper court. This is all because apparently Seka attacked the guards over his medication. This is what they've said. However, me and Billy and a few of the other lads have said that we'll be witnesses, but we're never called to be witnesses or to make a statement. I think they realise that they're flogging a dead horse, because Seka comes back with a sentence. He shows us the sentence, which we immediately give to Ali on a bit of string down below, and Ali just laughs. He said, "He's not allowed to go to the cinema for a month." We said, "Really?" "Yeah, no cinema for a month!" So they'd given him some sort of punishment that is completely irrelevant, because we don't have a cinema! So we laugh and joke and say that Seka is not allowed to watch the film in the evening. Seka believes us and for the first night he hides in the toilet while the film's on! Well, only for about half an hour, because I go and get him! I say, "Seka! Come on, don't be daft!" So he sits there watching the film with us laughing.

Friday

Billy and Marcel wake up about seven o'clock. They have breakfast with me, which is really quite nice, not that I'm eating breakfast, because we don't get any, but they had these bread rolls and Billy and Marcel decide to have a go at them. I pass, because of what they did to my stomach the last time. It's quite nice, the three of us getting up and having breakfast together. Billy is becoming more friendly with Marcel, so much so that they start weight training together. Marcel's shaken off the worst of the coming down off the cocaine. He's quite a normal guy now to speak to – he's still very arrogant, very full of himself, but at least he speaks a bit of English and that's good for Billy. I'm glad that if I do go home then at least Billy's got somebody to talk to.

When the guards come up for syem I ask to get Iggle Piggle's dressing changed as it'd bled through during the night in a couple of places. After much debate, they agree and off he goes. Ten minutes later they return and get me to go down with them down to see the doctor. Iggle Piggle lights up when I enter the room. The doctor has taken off the dressing and the wounds are all bleeding again, nowhere near like it was before though. He handed me the bandages and what I presumed was Iodine. I spent time closing up the wounds as best I could with thin strips of tape but really it all needed stitching properly; just make do I guess!! Repairs done we go back to the cell.

After lunch Billy and Marcel had a workout together, which was great for Billy and I think Marcel quite enjoyed it too. Billy's getting his mojo back, because it's nice to train with somebody, I guess. I didn't have the energy to train – I'd lost so much weight. Mentally and physically I wasn't in the right place to start lifting water bottles and hanging off upturned beds, plus I'm a bit of a chicken too, I didn't want to get caught by the guards and sent downstairs to solitary for exercising. Any form of exercise is strictly forbidden. Whereas Billy will break the rules a bit more than me. So I just sat quietly and watched them do it. Marcel's gelling well with Billy and they're training together, which is good news.

That evening, at about half past seven, the guards bring up my paperwork for court. They need my address and phone numbers. I'm a little bit confused because they've got all this information down below, but they want me to write out my address and phone numbers anyway. I ask them why and they say "procedure, procedure", yet again, procedure. A bit confused as to why I have court papers when I have a meeting planned with the judge I ask Ali, the Daesh lad from downstairs, who translates for me. Apparently I have court at 13:45 on the 29th in Bodrum. Okay, I understand that, but what am I supposed to do? I'm going to see the judge on the Tuesday or have I got court on the Friday, so I don't really know what's going on. He says it's court number one, the top level court, similar to The Old Bailey or so Billy tells me. Didn't sleep much and lay awake worrying about it all night, feeling seriously confused.

Chapter Seven

<u>Saturday 23rd</u>
Billy and Marcel get up at about half-six for breakfast. They take in the bread delivery, plus ten small pieces of feta cheese and six hard-boiled eggs. When I get up at about seven-ish Billy's fuming, really angry. We didn't know anything about these deliveries or this extra food. It seems that Medi's been stealing it. Normally it was one of the French lads that had been up all night, (they took it in turns), would take in the food, hide it away, then Medi would give it to the French lads later on in the day.

The usual, syem at about eight o'clock, then general rowing, general fighting about food for the rest of the day. This month can't finish soon enough for me. I'm so looking forward to the end, the court, that I find myself wishing my days away, which is something I've never done before. I keep mulling over that Green Day song, *Wake Me Up When September Ends*, and that's really what I want to do, just wake up when the month is finished. I do have happy days as well, usually Thursdays when I get to speak to the gang. When I think about them or I've spoken to them, I have a couple of songs in my head, a Placebo song, *Loud Like Love*, and The Killers, *Mr Bright Side* – there's a line in Mr Bright side "coming out of my cage" and it all seems a bit relevant at the moment.

<u>Sunday</u>
Billy and Marcel get up really early again, half-six-ish, and then they take in what's called the chicken soup. Apparently, when they

stirred it they found all these little bits of chicken breast in the bottom! Billy's just about to blow a blood vessel at this point. It looks like the same kind of chicken that the French lads fed the cat days ago. Billy removes all the chicken from the bottom of the soup pot and puts it in a bowl beside his bed and saves it for later! Of course, it's Sunday, more rows, more fights, just the usual stuff.

Monday morning

I'm really apprehensive and yet excited. I'm not sure whether I'm going to see the judge or not. Ever prepared I get ready, showered, dressed, just in case I do have to go and see the judge. I pretty much just end up sitting around waiting to see what happens, kind of doing my own head in.

The guards take both me and Iggle Piggle down to the doctor but guess what, no doctor. The guards indicate that I can re-bandage his arm without the doctor. They find all the stuff I had used before and I got on with it. The wounds looked better but two of them were still gaping. I closed them with tape as best as I could after smothering his arm in disinfectant, not a bad job for a bodge up. The guards seem pleased and I even get a pat on the back; then it's back to the cell.

Medi appears – he's completely out of cigarettes and announces that he's giving up. Well, from six hundred cigarettes a week down to nothing, this is going to be no mean feat for Medi. About four hours later the giving up thing is well and truly over, Medi's on the scrounge again, pestering everybody for cigarettes. He starts rowing with just about everybody. My flip-flop got broken in all the fights that broke out. When it all died down, I spent an hour or so putting it back together with string. If nothing else it occupied my time for the afternoon.

About half past four, Murat arrives and I called down to see him. Always smiling, always welcoming, he explains about court on Friday. I'm really nervous about court. Excited, but really worried too. Murat assures me. He says, "We're really sorry that you didn't get to see the judge today, but as your court was scheduled for Friday, there seemed little point in seeing him today." This was the judge's decision and not Murat's. I kind of disagreed with him – I'd like to have gone home a little bit sooner! However at this point, I'm just glad the end is in sight. Murat, bless him, just reassures me and tells me that everything's okay and everything is all prepared for Friday. Before he leaves he informs me that the maximum sentence for my crime is thirteen years but assures me that I will get nothing like that. Thirteen bloody years, you couldn't make it up!!! We go through my statement one more time. He just says to say what I need to say. Just tell the truth, because that's all that is relevant.

We talk a little bit about Billy. Murat explains that he's got to get permission from Billy's lawyer to enable him to speak to Billy in person. I think Billy's lawyer is being a little guarded, shall we say. Not much else happens for the rest of the day. The little owl comes and sees me again in the evening, putting me in a happy place before I sleep.

Tuesday

I get up and started my countdown again. I'm missing my music more than anything by now. Absolutely detest this Kral Pop. I think the lads just put it on to annoy me now! Yassar has managed to secure a meeting with his lawyer, which is some crazy-looking woman called Goolan, I'd seen her before during meetings with Murat. The Captain, who's Yassar's brother-in-law, becomes quite annoyed because they both have the same lawyer and yet only Yassar is going down to see Goolan. So when Yassar disappears out of the cell to his meeting, the Captain starts strutting around the cell, very annoyed. They don't really get on that well anyway. When Yassar does anything it's all about Yassar, he doesn't really care about anybody else, his own agenda.

Upon his return, Yassar then proceeds to tell everybody that he's managed to secure a phone call to his wife which he'll be getting next Thursday. On hearing this, the Captain goes absolutely berserk, which is pretty much the first time I've ever seen him react and get so angry. The poor guy hasn't spoken to his family in two years, so what do you expect?

Wednesday

I redress Iggle Piggle's arm again, no doctor yet again. The two wounds I was worried about were looking better and no signs of infection. Billy's still in a really good routine with his breakfast and his training with Marcel. He keeps telling me that he's going to miss me and it's going to be really empty when I've gone. I'm kind of like his big brother, almost his dad, I guess. I bought Billy's canteen again. I don't know whether it's a stupid move or not, but I've spent nearly all of the remaining money I had left in my account. I'm secretly hoping I'm going home! I bought four hundred cigarettes, shampoo, coffee, deodorant, and four phone cards to stock Billy up and give him a bit of breathing room after I've gone. Billy's only got seventy Turkish lira in his account, so he hasn't got much at all. He spends it all anyway. He's more into biscuits and chocolate, which you can buy, but I've never bothered to buy anything like that, just the basics for me. Still lots and lots of rows about food. Can't wait for Thursday, it can't come soon enough, when I get to talk to the gang.

<u>Thursday</u>

This is the last time I look at Iggle Piggle's arm and now we're down to plasters covering the two large wounds, all be it large plasters. I go down stairs for the second time on the Thursday morning – fantastic phone call with the guys. I tell them I'm really excited, really nervous, really scared but I'm looking forward to it. They already new about the maximum thirteen year sentence but didn't want to tell me. Hmmm!! They are all excited too and there is a feeling that we will all be back together soon. My last words to them were "see you later, love you, bye", which is our family goodbye.. Billy had a really good phone call with his dad and his nephews, then at the end he had a couple of minutes with Charlene to iron out the rows. The day just can't go fast enough.

That evening the guards call up telling me to be ready for half past seven Friday morning. Everyone's rushing around writing letters to their families. If I'm released, I can take all the letters with me. I've said I'll take them out – smuggle them down my boxers and then send them off to their loved ones, take a photo and WhatsApp them or e-mail them. I say make sure you put an address or phone number or something so that I can get your messages through. I went to bed around eleven, the little owl appeared as if on cue – to wish me good luck, I think! I was just nodding off when I heard a commotion at the entrance to the cell. I got up and peered down towards the gate. Two new cell mates were coming in with their mattresses. I got back into bed, they could wait until tomorrow.

Chapter Eight

<u>Friday 29th</u> September
Finally, the big day's here. I get up really early. I haven't had much sleep because I've been worrying about what's going to happen today. Pretty anxious, pretty nervous. Got to get myself ready for half-seven. Straight in the shower, freezing cold water, instantly awake now. Quick coffee. I get myself ready – I get my jeans on, Hamed's jeans, Medi's trainers, Medi's yellow jumper and I've got a T-shirt on underneath, an old white ambulance T-shirt. The two new lads are from Kazakhstan. One's asleep by the tv and the other is beside Marcel, sixteen men now in 40m2, it's crazy, welcome to the zoo!! They have both been caught smuggling refugees so Billy tells me.

I'm sitting there, expectant, ready and waiting, half-seven. Half-seven comes and goes. Then syem at eight o'clock comes and goes. Half-eight, now I'm nervously clock watching. Finally, at nine o'clock, they shout up to me: "Get ready! Get yourself ready!" I've been ready for an hour and a half, guys! They come up and get me. I've got all my paperwork, my statement and some other bits of paper that I've got for court.

A little bit stressed and anxious obviously, we go down the stairs. They search me; make sure I've got nothing. I've got a full packet of cigarettes – you're not allowed to take an open packet – but I've got a full packet of cigarettes with me, which I'd been advised to take by my cell mates . We go through the X-ray machine at the front. I have to take my belt off and anything metal, but the buttons on my jeans keep setting the alarm off, so I have to stand there holding the buttons. I walk through I don't know how many times, but eventually I get through. There I'm met by the gendarme, the military police, where they put the handcuffs on so tight it's ridiculous. I point it out, but they just laugh.

Then I'm put into a prison transport truck with four other guys, all in one cage. The other lads are all Turkish, I've never seen them before, but assume we're all going to the same court. We have a two hour journey, but they don't say anything to me at all. They just talk amongst themselves. By now the cuffs are digging in and I've got blood running down my hands. It's really hot in the truck, no ventilation. It's covered in graffiti, absolutely loads of graffiti, most of it in Arabic. Some of the lads are scraping their names into the walls with their handcuffs. There's a camera in the cage, but they don't seem to care too much. I just sit there quietly not daring to write anything on the walls.

Finally, after two hours, we get to Bodrum court. The truck's parked outside the front of the court. I recognise the building through the window when I stand up; I've been there before, it was the first court I went to way back when, six weeks ago when I was arrested at the airport. As we get out, we're grabbed, one gendarme on each arm, all armed to the teeth with assault rifles or AKs or whatever they are.

We're paraded – or I'm paraded mainly – in front of the press. There's lots of press there – twenty/thirty people – cameras, television cameras and all sorts. It's a bit of a media circus. The gendarme certainly seem to be putting on a big show for the cameras. Parade over, we get escorted down into this absolutely filthy, stinking cell. It stinks of cigarette smoke, smelly bodies and urine, it's vile. From there one by one we're taken to the toilet, still in cuffs. I use the toilet quickly, they smell worse than the cell. All the while the guards are standing about six inches from me while I'm having a wee, very off putting! It's obviously all a big show of strength. Back in the cell I sit and I wait. They come in with a bag with a banana and a roll, but they look like the same rolls we got in prison, so I steer clear of those! I eat the banana though. Then I have a few puffs on a cigarette to calm me down – the guards light it for you as you're not allowed your own lighter. One by one the four Turkish lads go off to court. They take their papers and off they go. As they come back one of them starts talking to me. He looks at my court papers and he wants to know (he has no proper English at all) why I'm going to Court 1; He can't believe I'm going to court 1. They're all going to court 2A, way down the levels, which makes me even more nervous than already am. Surely my alleged crime isn't fit for court 1. One by one they came back and I could vaguely understand that one had got two years, one had got six months.

They'd all got a sentence. So I'm waiting and worrying. I was supposed to be in there at 13:45, but 13:45 came and went and I just thought it's going to go on and on and on. Am I going to court? I was worrying, really fretting. Finally, at two o'clock they came and got me. They took my handcuffs off, but I didn't have a chance to wipe all the blood off my hands. Yet again, a big show, one on each arm, they walked me down the corridor and finally into the court room. They placed me in the dock and then one guard stood either side of me. Behind me was the press. There were only about five members of the press there I think. One looked like an artist with his sketch pad (I don't know if he was a portrait artist). The other four looked like reporters – they had press badges.

To my left, as I'm facing the judge, there was my translator who introduced herself in perfect English, which was a very welcome relief. She was lovely, absolutely lovely. To my right was Murat, my solicitor, who was standing there smiling. He gave me a sense of confidence, which was very reassuring. In front of me was a large polished wooden structure with five people who all looked like judges, all wearing robes sitting in a row facing me. One very smart man in the middle who was the main judge, then there were two other assistant judges either side of him. The man on the far right was the prosecutor and on the far left was somebody taking notes I believe. It all seemed to be very formal and very serious.

The judge, speaking through my translator, asks me to begin my story. Very politely and humbly I said, "Where would you like me to start?" as I didn't want to get anything wrong. He asked me would it be better if he asked the questions? "Yes, that would be great," I said. I'm really nervous, I've got a really dry mouth and I'm trying to remember Murat's instructions. Murat had said to mention these four things, Tobe, whatever you do, don't forget to mention the four things. We go through the story very thoroughly. I simply tell the truth, I even managed to remember the four things that I have to include! The judge seems pretty pleased with what I've said. I answer openly, honestly. Murat is giving me the nod every now and then to keep my confidence up, I guess.

An expert from the Bodrum museum hired by the prosecution explains that the coins are Roman, made of bronze and amazingly have a historical value of £15,000. He goes on to say that they have great historical significance to Turkey but his story falls flat through cross examination by Murat and the Judge where he finally confesses that the coins real value monetary value is between £5 and £10 and were probably purchased on an online auction site such as Ebay!!! What?? You've got to be kidding me, I've been held for six weeks in maximum security for coins worth £10, it beggars belief. It just seems to make the whole thing even more ridiculous than it already is. The expert goes on to say that the coins are now on display with my name written underneath the exhibit. Honestly, you couldn't make it up!!

After I've finished answering all the questions Murat sums up. He makes a simple speech which is translated to me. In it he also points out that the captain of the boat had offered to come to court on my behalf and reinforce my statement. The judge had not felt that this was necessary and the captain was spared the trip to court.

Finally, the judge says that's enough, thank you very much. They have a little chat amongst themselves, at which point my heart's in my mouth, my stomach is on spin cycle. The judge turns to the translator and says something in Turkish. My translator turns to me and says: "Toby, you are hereby released without charge. You are a free man. However, if you re-offend in Turkey within five years, you will have a thirteen month prison sentence and a 2,400 Turkish lira fine." I didn't really expect this. I thought I'd just either be sentenced or released. So I answered back: "Will I actually have a criminal record?" I was really, really worried about having a criminal record because it might come back and haunt me when I go back to work on the ambulance back in the UK. I think they were a bit taken aback at my question and started talking amongst themselves. At which point Murat, intervened and said, "Look, Toby, this is a really good deal. You will have no criminal record and you can go home today. Are you in agreement?" I said, "Well, what do you think?" He said, "It's a really good deal and the only deal on offer, go for it!" So reluctantly I said, ''okay fine, I am happy to accept.'' If this was the only way to get home then this was what I had to accept.

With that, it was all wrapped up, it was all over, a massive relief. I remember just slumping forward with tears rolling down my face. I was just elated, absolutely elated. Completely exhausted as well. The gendarme then opened the dock for me and rather than the heavy handed approach gestured for me to step down from the dock, a completely different scenario now. They're letting me move around without holding me. It was a little bit weird. I walked straight over to the translator and shook her hand and gave her a huge hug which I don't think was the done thing but I was so elated. I said thank you very much, you were fantastic. She had a tear or two as well, she knew the judge had made the right decision. Then I walked over to Murat and gave him a great big hug. I had a few more tears, as did Murat. This guy was absolutely amazing. I can't recommend him highly enough. If ever you're in trouble in Turkey then that's the man to have. He's an amazing guy, who can't do enough for you. I would love to have a beer and chat with him one day well away from these settings. I approached the bench – I didn't know whether to shake hands with them – so in the end I just said thank you very much. I put my hands together, for some reason, almost like I was praying. I just nodded at them and said thank you very much. That seemed to go down well and I got a nod back from the judge.

Murat explained that after he had signed the relevant papers he would come and get me from Mugla prison and take me to the airport. I would be flying home tonight, amazing news. This was really hard to take in, my head was spinning at the thought of seeing Heidi and the boys!!

The gendarme gestured for me to follow them. I went out and as we were walking back through the corridors towards the cell, they were patting me on the back! The gendarme! These are the guys that had me in cuffs and made my wrists bleed on the way in but now it was completely different. Really hard for me to work out. Then as we're walking down the corridor they're high-fiving me! "Well done! Well done! You're free! You're free!" Whoa! Crazy! Spinning my head out completely! We got outside and the four Turkish lads were already in the truck. As I approached the truck they pushed me towards the driver's seat. It was like a big joke because now I was free I could drive back to Mugla! They were laughing and joking. Anyway, joke over, I was placed back into the cage inside the truck. I was quiet all the way back deep in thought, trying to process what had just happened.

I didn't really talk to the Turkish lads much. I explained as best I could in pigeon Turkish/pigeon English that I was free and I was going home and I was very, very excited. Although I was handcuffed now they were really, really loose. I could almost get my hands out of them they were that loose. It was a great feeling. It was a long journey back, but it was a great feeling, knowing that I'd be going home soon. All my feelings were amplified by ten, very emotional but the biggest one was that of massive relief, a sense of peace. Finally, somebody had listened to what I'd said and believed what I'd said and the result was, I was free and finally going home.

We finally arrived back at Mugla prison after about two hours. I was searched on the way in yet again, the usual stuff. I walked down the corridor and back up to my cell. As I arrived upstairs all the lads were hanging around the gate all asking, "How'd you get on? How'd you get on?" I said, "Lads, I'm free! I'm going home!" They were all cheering and applauding. It was absolutely lovely.

Quite emotional though, still trying to hold it all in. I got inside the cell composing myself and said, "Lads, get all your letters, I need all your letters." So off they went running around getting their letters ready.

After about twenty minutes the guards appeared and I realised I was still wearing everybody else's kit, so I quickly changed and put my shorts and T-shirt back on. Medi said to keep the jumper, so I kept the jumper. I was grateful because it was really quite cold at night and thought I looked good in it. I stuffed seven letters and my diary, down my boxer shorts, but by now my denim shorts were hanging off me, they were really loose, even my boxers were really loose, so I was a little bit worried about these letters as they'd given me so many, I was worried they'd fall out! I took my wallet, my photos, my toothbrush, an extra T-shirt, an extra pair of boxers and a pair of shorts that Billy had given me. Everything else I left in my locker for Billy.

I said goodbye to everyone. It was really hard saying goodbye to Billy. I didn't want to leave him behind. That was quite emotional. Big man-hug. Billy was saying, "I'm going to miss you so much, bruv," in his Essex accent! Before I left I said goodbye to Hamed. They'd confiscated his watch because it was digital, they were worried he could send e-mails and access the internet on it. So I took my old Seiko off and gave it to him. He was absolutely elated. It's very hard not knowing the time in prison. All the hours seem to roll into one unless you've got some idea of the time. He was really made up so I got a big man-hug off Hamed as well! As I left Sag Terras M1-11, all the lads were cheering and clapping. I think that started a chain reaction as the terrorists below us and even the Feto terrorists, down the bottom all began cheering. There were probably about eighty people all clapping and applauding.

Even the prison guards who came to pick me up and take me down, they were patting me on the back and shaking my hand. It was a really nice feeling. It was a feeling that I'd won, justice had been done finally and people were genuinely happy that I was going home. We walked down the stairs and all these letters were moving around in my boxers. I was absolutely pooping myself! Although I was officially free I didn't want to cause myself any unnecessary trouble by getting caught smuggling out these bloody letters! I just wanted to get out of there! Fortunately, they stayed in my shorts. We got down to the bottom of the stair well and standing by the desk was Mahmood, the only guard that had ever showed me any compassion. I walked over to him and said I was free. I think he already knew anyway. We had a big man–hug, touching heads the Turkish way and thanked him so much for looking after me while I was in Mugla.

And then off I went, down towards the reception desk where I'd come in the first night. The senior guard there shook my hand then invited me round the other side – I had to put my hand on the fingerprint machine, just to check it was the right person going out, I guess. I had to give them back my prison ID, which secretly I wanted to keep. I sat in a little room for a minute while they sorted out the paperwork and then they came and got me and made me stand outside the manager's office where I had met the British consul the first time. I waited there for a couple of minutes. The little bald twat, as I had come to call him, he invited me in, finally. He looked me up and down as though I was still a piece of shit he'd found on the bottom of his shoe. He made a big deal about signing the paperwork, checking it through I don't know how many times. It was a big game, a big show. Just him flexing his muscles, I guess. Small man syndrome. The senior guard who was in there with me, he came over, shook my hand and said good luck in English. As I went to shake the little bald man's hand, he tried to take it away, tried to withdraw it. I don't think he wanted to shake my hand at all. Quick as you like I grabbed it. He refused to clasp my hand or wrap his fingers around and kept his hand very straight, but I squeezed the life out of it! It was like my final fuck off! Very childish but it felt so good!!

We left his office and I was escorted back through the main doors, through the X-ray machine. They started giving me my stuff back – my man-bag, my chargers, my e-cigarette. The only things they didn't give me was my passport and driving licence. I questioned this and one of the guards said ''I have it, I'm holding this''. So I thought okay, well hand it over, that's what I need! I'm not leaving the country without it but he kept hold of it. I was escorted through the main doors, out into the yard, where this guard promptly gave my stuff to two policemen. I thought where's Murat? So I asked, I said: "Where's Murat, my lawyer?" These two policemen in uniform in a police car, they said: "No, no, no. Hospital first." I thought okay, fair enough, I get this – procedure, yet again.

Off we go to a hospital I've never been before. We walk in. Same scenario though: "Have you any hurt?" "No." Back in the car. All blue lights and off we go again. I said, "Where are we going now?" They said, "We're going to the police station." I thought okay, fair enough, more paperwork, more procedure. It's quite a long drive to the police station, probably about an hour or so. We just seem to be going out into the middle of rural Turkey. There are no houses or buildings, just open space. We finally arrive at this compound – big gates, barbed wire. The funniest looking police station I've ever seen. We drive through the gates and come up to the front door, where there were a couple of guards dressed in brown this time. They didn't look like police, they looked more like a private security company. One of the fellas had pretty good English, or at least probably the best I'd encountered. I said, "Where's my lawyer? I need my lawyer." He said, "Why do you need your lawyer?" I said, "I'm going home, I'm free." He looked at me really blankly. I said, "Why am I here?" He got his phone out and went onto Google Translate. He showed me his phone, which said ''you've committed a crime''. I said, "I'm a free man, I don't have to be here anymore. I'm supposed to be meeting my lawyer and going home on a plane tonight." I'm really, really confused. I don't really know what to do. I grab a cigarette, light it up, and just sit outside on one of the benches, just hanging around while they talk amongst themselves.

Finally, twenty/thirty minutes later Murat arrives. He apologises profusely. He said he got delayed with paperwork at Bodrum court. He said, "Toby, you're booked on a flight, half-past one in the morning, it's all good." Fantastic news. It seems that these guards had been waiting for some sort of manager of this facility or centre. The manager arrived – very slick-looking young man, not a hair out of place kind of guy. Murat and I get shown into a little office just inside the main door. The manager then says: "There's no release today, you can't be signed out of here until Monday." At this point Murat loses his cool. He doesn't explode but you can see he's pretty irate and annoyed. They have an argument for what lasts for probably twenty minutes, it gets pretty heated, so much so that I go outside and have another cigarette while they're sorting it out. I can hear them rowing inside. Obviously Murat is not pleased at all. Finally, Murat comes out and he says that this slimy little guy won't budge. It's procedure, I have to stay in this detention centre for the weekend, but he promises faithfully – apparently he's sworn on the Koran, whatever that means – that I will be leaving on Monday and Murat will come back on Monday and pick me up.

So what's gone from this massive high, knowing that I'm going home, that I'd been released, it's been such a good day in lots of ways, has turned into yet another disappointment. I say to Murat, "Can I use your phone really quick and phone Heidi to let her know that I'm okay?" Murat gives me his phone, I call Heidi and we have a long chat, probably ten/fifteen minutes at least. I explain what's happened, that I'm free and I should have been going home but I've got to stay in this place until Monday. She's upset obviously, I'm upset, but I think we're both wondering what sort of guarantee there is on Monday, both living in hope. I give Murat his phone back after the telephone conversation. One of the detention centre guards comes out, a lady, she tries to reassure me and says this place is nothing like Mugla Prison. It's like a hotel. The food is good, you have hot and cold water, it's okay. I'm thinking okay, fair enough. I don't want to push anybody's buttons. So I say goodbye to Murat and in I wander.

Chapter Nine

I enter the detention centre where they take my all my belongings, even my wedding ring. The only thing they allow me to keep is some money which was given to me as I was leaving the prison – it was obviously what was left over in my canteen/prison account. There wasn't much there at all – about 30 Turkish lira. That and the change of clothes were all I was allowed to keep. I went into the lobby area where there was an X-ray machine. I went through the X-ray machine and was escorted down the corridor. I don't think they really knew what to do with me or where to put me. They looked into lots of different cells and finally we walked back up the same corridor and opened door number three, they said you stay here. One of the guards came in with me, a female. She walked around and checked the place over.

It was completely empty. Sixteen bunk beds and sixteen lockers. There were two showers and a hole in the floor toilet. It was all quite nice really, basic, but a million times better than Mugla. The only thing I asked her was is there any shampoo? She said no, you can buy shampoo when you go for your meals. Okay, fair enough. She went off and came back with some bed linen. I was given a towel, a pillow, a pillow case, a sheet and a duvet cover, which was like heaven to me because I hadn't had anything. It was really, really nice. They left, locked the door, and yet again I felt just like a prisoner, some bloody hotel this was! At least I had a comfortable bed and bed linen. Immediately I stripped off and went to the shower, turned the water on where there was hot and cold running water. It was fantastic. Once I got into the shower cubicle there was a big bottle of shampoo on the window sill outside. You could reach through the bars, so I grabbed this bottle – I don't know whose it was and didn't really care, it smelled great though. I showered two, three times and washed my hair two or three times and just washed all of Mugla down the drain. I also washed my T-shirt, my shorts and my boxers with the shampoo. It was amazing, just so nice to have a proper shower. I hung all my clothes up to dry on the ends of all the other bunk beds and basically just chilled out. It was so, so quiet, no noise at all. Where I'd been used to this menagerie in Mugla with people screaming and crying and shouting and praying all the time, it was dead quiet. I could hear a few voices but it was lovely. Very weird, very strange, very different, but great nonetheless.

I don't know what time it was because I've got no watch now, but the door opened and I was escorted into a mess hall/canteen. I stood there at the back of the queue – there were only a couple of people ahead of me. There were lots of tables with people sitting at them – men, women, children – all looked to be Arabs. I stood there and waited my turn in the queue for some food. When I got to the food itself it just looked awful, worse than Mugla. In the end, I ended up taking a bottle of water and walked out. The guards approached me and said don't you want food? No, no mate! It just looked awful. They put me in the exercise yard 3A, which was next to my cell.

There was a ping pong table there. The yard was probably six by four metres – a nice big space in which I could walk around in. I walked around for a bit, had a few puffs on a cigarette. Probably fifteen minutes later they put me back in my cell. I went straight to the shower, had another shower, and then lay on my bed. I just laid there in silence thinking over what had happened and why I was here. Frustration and disappointment yet again, but also knowing that I'd actually been released by the court, was a real boost. I kept hearing some really weird scratching noises. I wondered if the place was haunted because the walls were breeze blocks, they were really thick, yet I could identify these really, really clear sounds of scratching. I searched the place from top to bottom looking for a mouse or a rat. It sounded human, it sounded odd. I kept thinking this place is haunted! I'd tried to get into the lights on the ceiling to pull the bulbs out, it was so bright in the cell but they were padlocked to the ceiling, so I didn't manage to get any bulbs out. Nonetheless, I laid on my bed, closed my eyes and slept like an absolute log, I was exhausted.

Early Saturday morning, at about three in the morning, I could hear the familiar sounds of people praying, right outside my window in the exercise yard. I got up and walked towards the window where I could see four lads in the yard praying away. I pulled all the windows shut, closed them all up, and then went back to bed. Half past seven, I got called out of the cell for breakfast. I know it was half past seven because there was a clock on the wall outside the cell, so as I walked past I got some idea of the time. Breakfast looked appalling, absolutely rubbish. It was bread, but an uncut loaf, somebody had cut it, but I think they'd put all their weight on it while they were cutting it. It looked like dough balls and looked really unappetising. So I thought I'd give it a miss, all I took was a cup of chai and a bottle of water. I bought a phone card and then left. The guards were saying, "No breakfast, no breakfast!" No thank you, mate. They didn't seem overly concerned though.

They locked me in the exercise yard where I spent approximately two hours. I just walked and walked and walked, round and round this exercise yard in my flip flops that were held together with string by now as they'd fallen apart in prison. I took my T-shirt off as it was beginning to get really warm. I just wandered round and round this yard, so much so that by the time I'd finished my trek, my legs and my hips were aching. Where I hadn't been moving for six weeks, I'd just sat still, sedentary for six weeks, everything was aching, but it was so nice to move around properly and do a bit of exercise. The lads who were in cell number four adjacent to my exercise yard, which was their exercise yard too it transpires – kept calling "English, English" but I just ignored them, walked past them. They were calling to me through these barred windows on their cell, but I ignored them and walked round as though I couldn't hear them.

Finally, after my little walk around the exercise yard, the guards came and got me. As I'm walking towards my cell, I noticed the payphone on the wall and I said, "Can I just make a quick call?" They agreed and let me phone. I get my phone card out and pop it in the wall and dial Heidi on her mobile. She answers immediately, which is great, and she explains that they've just been to the school fete and that the boys had won me a coconut, of all things. I'm missing them all so much. It was a really nice call. They were sitting on a bench in the sunshine having a family day. I was more than a little bit gutted that I couldn't have been there, but I can't wait until Monday. Heidi asks me what I want to eat when I get home. Nothing with rice I say but anything else goes. A bottle of Old Peculiar wouldn't go amiss either.

Lunch –you'll never guess, rice and beans, yet again. I'm so hungry now because I've only had a banana since Thursday, so I'm absolutely ravenous. Lots of foreign men, and boys. They all seem to be male. No talking to anybody. I sat on my own and ate my rice and beans. When I'd finished I walked out and the guards put me in a different exercise yard – exercise yard number four. I was pushed through the door. The guards gave me two cigarettes, because they hold the cigarettes for you, it was all a bit weird. As soon as I went in there, there was a crowd of people who came over to me. "You're English, you're English!" They all wanted to know everything. Of course, they didn't speak brilliant English, so I explained what I knew about what was going on in the world, what I'd learnt from CNN Turk, because there's no television in this place, and what I'd seen in the papers. That conversation went on for a good half an hour or so. They explained that they were all refugees. They were from all different Arab countries – Iran, some from Yemen, Syrians – and they were basically all families that had tried to come to Turkey or Greece and had been caught without paperwork or passports, and were being detained awaiting deportation back to their own countries. They told me the prisoners in cell four were Daesh terrorists and that was why I was in their yard and not mine. The guards had to keep us apart.I went from there back to my room where I had a snooze.

I woke up to that scratching sound again and spent ten minutes looking for the ghost! I had another shower before dinner – rice and beans – then back to yard number four with the refugees. Another chat, a few puffs on a cigarette, went back to my room and slept all night. Really, really quiet.

<u>Sunday morning</u>
Breakfast – chai and water, no food – and then this time I went back to exercise yard number three. I wandered around for a short while. I was only in there very briefly, then the guards came and got me. They put me back in my cell, but they took me through a different door this time; a door connecting my cell to the exercise

yard. Before they locked it I managed to shove a bit of paper, Heidi's mobile number, in the lock, so when they thought they'd locked it, it hadn't locked properly.

As soon as the guards disappeared I opened the door and wandered back into the exercise yard where there were now four lads in there. I'd already figured out that I wasn't supposed to be with these guys because we were kept well apart. When I was in the yard they left and vice versa. They introduced themselves to me. They came over and started talking to me. They were quite threatening to start off with: "Why are you in our yard? Why are you doing this? You're English." They were just in my face. I explained that I'd been in Mugla prison and I was not scared of them. Deep inside I was shaking like a leaf, but the same old front, show no fear! Once they had reeled their necks in they confessed that they, these four men were all Daesh or ISIS terrorists awaiting deportation back to their own countries. So that's the reason for keeping us apart. The one with the really good English was a guy called Al Mohamed. He was from Yemen. There was another fella, who's English wasn't so bad, called Hassan and he was from Syria. The other two – one was Russian, with no English and one was a crazy-looking guy! He looked like an evil cartoon character! Really dodgy-looking little guy. I don't know where he came from. He didn't say much at all, but he was always watching you. Pretty scary bunch, but I showed no fear. I had a little bit of a row with the scary one, but he backed off and I backed off.

After about an hour or so, we were chatting away and they seemed to quite like me really. They had a tea flask and they offered me tea and cigarettes and it was all quite amicable. A little bit surreal really, tea with terrorists. I chatted with them and asked, "Are you convicted terrorists?" Al Mohamed, he refused, he said,

"No, I'm not a terrorist, I'm a businessman from Istanbul. I have businesses there." Hassan said he was caught with bomb-making equipment, but it wasn't his, he was holding it for somebody else, although he was still convicted as a terrorist. They pointed to the Russian guy and said that he was just caught buying nuts and bolts and started laughing loudly. Yeah, really bloody funny lads!! Idiots!! It was all a big joke to them. I said what about the scary one? They said he was caught with a suicide vest and things like that. Okay, fair enough, don't push too hard! So there I was with at least three Daesh terrorists! I don't know about number four, I don't think any of them were telling me the whole truth anyway.

With that the guards come in and they're a little bit shocked that we're all together. I point out that the lock was broken and that I had access to this room. I pointed out that we're all getting on okay, so let's leave it. Reluctantly they kind of agreed. So then my door was left open all day and I could come and go into the exercise yard as I pleased, which was really nice. At one point in the afternoon we all got pushed into my cell and the door was locked, although not really because my bit of paper was still stuffed in the lock. Some workmen came in and fitted a basketball hoop on the far end. The Daesh terrorist lads were all very excited about it! At which point I pointed out you might have a basketball hoop but you've got no ball! The excitement soon died down! Then I had lunch with the four Daesh lads and then back into the exercise yard again for the afternoon.

Hassan picked up on the fact that I was in Mugla and he asks me if I was in the foreign cell. I said ''yes, of course, Sag Terras M1-11.'' His eyes lit up and he said do you know The Captain? I said yeah, yeah, I know The Captain. He said do you know Yasser? I said, yeah, yeah, they're brother-in-laws. He said yes that's right! It transpires that Hassan was on the same ship as both The Captain and Yasser. He asks me lots of questions about them and their well being and we chat about them for a while. It transpires that Hassan had left the prison under the impression that he was being released – released back into the Turkish population, which is quite amusing because that just doesn't happen. Anyway somewhere along the line he was then caught with bomb–making equipment. I don't know when he got turned or when he got brainwashed or whatever happened, but he was now in this detention centre awaiting deportation back to Syria.

Then we all go to dinner together. After dinner, our rice and beans, we go back to the yard. Hassan makes me some tea, they seem to get the hot water from the canteen. They've obviously bought teabags so they make the tea in an old plastic Pepsi bottle, wrap it in an old blanket to keep the heat in and then share it amongst themselves throughout the evening. Although they've got a bad background, they seem to be quite different from the Mugla guys, because they will share. The Mugla guys didn't have that concept at all, but these were almost European in the way they acted.

Finally, we get escorted back to our respective cells. At which point I have yet another shower, I can't get enough of those! Then into bed and off I go to snoozeland, off to sleep. I was sleeping like a log when I hear this bang on the window. There's a guard banging on the window from the exercise yard. I'm standing there in my boxer shorts thinking what on Earth does he want? Everything's dark – outside it's pitch black. There's a small light on in the exercise yard, but that's it. He's banging on the window and he's got a cigarette in his hand. I said, "What do you want, mate? What's the time?!" He showed me his phone it was 3:13. I said, "Why are you waking me up at 3.13?" and offering me a cigarette he said, "You smoke, you smoke!" Now I'm totally confused!? Anyway, he gave me a cigarette and told me to stand as close as I could to the bars and blow the smoke out of the window so as not to set the fire alarm off in my cell. So I lit the cigarette, wondering what the hell's going on when the four Daesh lads appear in the exercise yard and get down and start praying. It's just so surreal! I don't know to this day why he woke me up and offered me a cigarette, but he did! I had my cigarette and watched the Daesh lads pray for a bit and then went back to bed.

I got up normal time, half past seven. Breakfast with the Daesh lads and then back to the yard. The manager appears, the slimy little guy that I'd met on the Friday evening, he goes absolutely ballistic at the guards, saying that I should not be with these Daesh terrorists and it was not good at all. At which point I intervened and said I've been with them all of yesterday, we're getting on okay, there's no trouble, no aggression, no hint of any violence at all. He calms down and leaves us in the exercise yard. So we're mingling around, chatting away in the exercise yard when four more guys come into the exercise yard and these turn out to be yet another four Daesh terrorists, one of which had been to Bristol and he was an avid Bristol City supporter! He kept walking round the yard, looking at me for approval, shouting "Bristol City"! What a head-spin! It was just nuts. We're in the middle of nowhere, in the middle of this detention centre, with a Daesh terrorist shouting Bristol City!

I asked the guards: "It's Monday, I'm supposed to be going home, where's my lawyer?" One of the guards with the good English comes over and says: "In about one hour you will go and see your lawyer. He's already here, he's having a chat with the manager and sorting out your release." This is great news! Huge sense of relief. Things are happening. Fantastic. Sure enough, after about an hour, I get escorted into the front office and there's Murat greeting me with a big hug. He said, "How are you doing? Have you been okay?" He was really worried about my welfare. I said, "Yeah, it's all good, I'm happy, we're going home?" He said, "Yeah, yeah, we're leaving here at three o'clock." I said, "Do I have to go back to the cell?" He said, "Yeah, but stay with me here for half an hour and we can walk outside in the compound." So I walked outside with Murat and we chatted for twenty minutes/half an hour until the guards come and get me and take me back to the cell.

Roll on three o'clock! About half past two, I get called to the front. Murat's there again and he explains that we'll be leaving in a police car. We of course have to go to the hospital first to get checked and make sure that I have no hurt, and then from there we'll go to the airport. Okay, great, I can accept all that. Then Murat turns to me and says, "You know, Toby, I had two goals." I said, "What were they then?" He said, "One was to get you released with no criminal charges and the other one was to get you home in time for your birthday." I said, "Oh, that's strange." He said, "You know, in time for your birthday." I said, "Oh yeah, but when's that?" He said, "Your birthday, it's tomorrow." "Really?" And then it struck me. I had no idea of time or dates or anything. I'd completely forgotten about my birthday, put it to the back of my mind, it was crazy. The fact that I didn't know made me really quite sad. Not that I celebrate my birthdays massively! At fifty three you kind of forget them! It was just another head-spin.

Murat then explains that he's going to follow me in his car. We are just about to leave and I said to Murat, "I just need to check. Have we got my driving licence, my bank cards, and my passport?"

The police wouldn't let me have my passport back and they'd left my driving licence on the photocopier, which really helpful. So off we go, straight to the hospital. Have you any hurt? No, no hurt. I get signed off, then back in the car and off we go. Just before we leave, in fact, Murat gets the police to take a photo of both of us standing outside the hospital. It's a photo that he can send to Heidi to show that I'm actually on my way – I'm actually heading towards the airport. I get back into the police car.

Murat's following me in his wife's car because his is in for a service, so he's trying to keep up with these lads on blue lights in his wife's Vauxhall Astra! I keep looking out of the back window, looking at Murat – a white knuckle ride chasing a police car! It does make me giggle. I asked the police can I plug my phone in and charge it up and see if I can get a signal so that I can speak to Heidi. I plug my phone into the front and my e-cigarette into the back charger. My iTunes automatically connects to their stereo and the Muse album Absolution loads up on the display. *Absolution*, I couldn't believe it, out of all the albums on my phone it had to be that one. Now I knew that I was going home. Absolution, it made me very emotional, it's an amazing album, even the police liked it. So off we go, on our way to Dalaman Airport.

They've explained that I couldn't go on a flight that has any connections, ie. a stopover in Istanbul, it's got to be a direct flight. Dalaman is a lot closer to wherever the hell we were, only an hour's drive away. I'm getting a little bit nervous because time's ticking on

Chapter Ten

We arrive at Dalaman Airport. I'm super excited now. Finally, I'll be getting on a plane and leaving this godforsaken country. While I was in the police car I found a coin in my bag that Brody had found while he was snorkelling! It was only a Turkish lira but by now I was completely paranoid and never wanted to see another Turkish coin in my life. It was a bit crusty and copper content had gone green. I think it was still relevant currency but I'm paranoid, so I finished my bottle of water quick as you like, pushed it into the bottle of water, put the lid on and as I walked into the airport, I found the nearest bin and chucked it in.

One policeman and Murat, follow me in, the other policeman parks the car. Murat's on double yellow lines, but I don't think he seems to care much. In we go. Murat explains to me that it's better if I check-in on my own so as not to draw attention to myself with the police and everything else. They hang back and almost hide behind this great big pillar! Pegasus Airlines, what a sight for sore eyes they are. Murat's given me my ticket. I walk over with my passport and show the lady behind the desk. No tricky questions, just the usual, have you any bags etc. She hands me my boarding pass and I wander back over to Murat. I've got seat 1A – I've never had seat 1A before. How I ended up with seat 1A who knows.

The other policeman joins us with the airport police. They have a conversation, explaining my situation, then they wave me over where I'm handed over to the airport police. Although Murat is still hanging around, I'm with the airport police now and they take me through the X-ray and put my bag through the machine. All completely normal so far. The airport policemen walk me through to passport control. I hand over my passport and boarding card to the passport control and wait. The passport officer starts gesticulating wildly, I thought he was going to blow a fuse. He didn't know what to do. He was flapping and panicking and talking to the guy in the booth next door, then asking the policemen loads of questions. He opened my passport at the page that said that I'd arrived in Turkey and I'd already left Turkey. He didn't really know what to do. In the end, I said can't you just void it, because you've got all this paperwork here from the courts, the police, and everything else, just void it and stamp me in and stamp me out again on the same day or something. He seemed to like this idea and pretty much did just that.

I finally clear passport control, still accompanied by the airport police, when Murat and the original two policemen that had driven me to the airport started shouting at me, "Come back! Come back!" I thought, oh my God, what have I done now? I walked back through all of the X-ray machines, set every alarm off you can imagine to find out that all they want is a photo for Heidi! So they take this photograph of me, smiling and waving like a fool. I give Murat a big hug and then policemen want a hug too, very strange, to say the least. I thanked Murat so much for all he's done, and with a tear in my eye I said goodbye to him. As I turned round I realised that every security officer in the airport was running at me because I'd just probably broken every rule there was by walking back through all the X-rays. The airport police get me out of a sticky situation and explain to security why I'd done what I did.

Off we wander towards the gate. The policeman explains: "You have now fifteen minutes for take-off, so you have to run!" So me and this policeman end up running through the airport to get to the gate. Finally I get to the gate – it's full of people, obviously all waiting to get on the plane. This policeman, who had been quite friendly before, now turned into some sort of authoritative big man . . . it was all a big show yet again . . . where he proceeded to search me from head to toe, arms out wide, assume the position yet again, in front of everybody, the whole departure lounge! The other passengers were all looking at me probably thinking I was some sort of hardened criminal. I didn't really care, I really didn't. All I wanted to do was get on the plane. After my pat down, I was whisked onto the plane before anybody else. The policeman walked me down the ramp, handed me over to the air stewardess who put me in seat 1A where I sat in anticipation.

Everybody got on the plane, all looking at me strangely, after the fiasco search that I'd just been through, wondering who the hell I was. I remember sitting in this big seat with loads of leg room just so, so happy to finally be on an aeroplane. Later on during boarding, a lady comes and sits next to me, seat 1B. She doesn't say anything to me and I don't say anything to her. The plane backs out and finally lifts off. As it lifts off I have a few tears. I'm not crying like a girl, but I've got tears and I'm so relieved, so pleased to be leaving the country. Finally on my way home.

As soon as we're up in the air and the fasten seat belt signs are switched off, the lady sitting next to me moves across one seat to 1C. I'm inwardly thinking perhaps it's because I stink! I've been in all these weird places and I probably don't smell too fresh. My beard's really long, my hair's really long, I look like the Wild Man of Borneo. She's probably thinking I'll move over a seat just to keep distance from this guy! She turns to me, she seems quite nice and starts chatting. Immediately my guard goes up and I think she's press. She wants to talk to me. I'm absolutely paranoid at this point.

She asks me if my name's Toby and then all my alarm bells go off. I said, "Yes, yes, my name's Toby." She said she recognised me from the British press and twigged it was me when I got searched in the departure lounge. She said that she'd been over for her friend's wedding but had to cut her holiday short because of a family crisis and she's on her way home now. She says she works for a recruitment agency in London. I don't tell her anything at all, except that my name's Toby, I was a prisoner in Mugla, and pretty much nothing else. However, she does most of the talking. She's a proper chatterbox. Her name's Stephanie. She was lovely, absolutely lovely lady. She asked me if I'd like a drink. I decline, I say no thank you, very British. She's got the menu in front of her and she says she definitely needs a drink. She said if she buys two rosé wines, she can get two beers for free. So she buys the two wines and the next thing I know I've got two beers, which I was very grateful for. The first one didn't touch the sides, but I sipped the second one slowly. It was Effes Turkish beer, but it was still quite nice. I explained to her that I'm a little bit worried about going home and the reaction from the press at the airport. I asked her did I smell like a dead badger and she handed me over a little deodorant, so I gratefully had a little spray of deodorant underneath my arms and just immediately felt cleaner.

The plane lands after the fastest four hours ever- must have been all her chattering. She's a little bit squishy by now. I think the wine's gone to her head. We depart the aeroplane and head down towards baggage reclamation. She showed me through the electronic passport thing, which I'd never done before, much faster, we flew through there. She says she's got some bags to pick up. I said I've got nothing, so we say our goodbyes. I doubt I'll ever meet her again, but she was lovely. It was nice to talk to an English person and find out a little bit about what's been going on in the UK. She gave me a great big hug and I think we both had a few tears, it was quite emotional.

I was just so, so glad to be back on British soil. I thought about doing the Pope thing and kissing the ground but I resisted! There I was, on my own, no guards and no police. I walked towards the green channel. No sign of any Customs guys at all. Not that I had anything to declare. As I walked through the green channel I saw the two sets of doors. One opened and then the other one opened and all I could see was my two boys and that was it, I had tunnel vision all I could see was my two wonderful boys. I know inside I was worried about the press and I was hoping to God they weren't there, but I didn't really care now. All I could see was my boys. I walked through and just ran to them. Picked them up. Great big cuddles, what a feeling. Then I was on my knees, hugs, kisses, crying like a girl really. I look up and see Heidi, I stand up and we hug, kiss, like we are the only ones in the world, just a massive relief. Then I see Zoe and Zach, lots of hugs. Everyone's crying, everyone's in tears, but finally we get it all together. To this day I don't know if there were any press there or not, but we basically just leg it out of the arrivals lounge and head to the car.

I just remember leaving the airport, thinking thank you God that I finally got home. It was just incredible to finally be home after forty five days of hell. Coming out of the airport I hear this phsssss in the back of the car, the boys had taken the top off an Old Peculiar, my favourite beer! They passed the bottle through and I had my first sip of English beer. So there I am, back on British soil, with my family, drinking beer in the car on the way home from Gatwick airport. They'd made me a sausage and bacon sandwich, which I didn't eat because I was too excited. I'm just so excited and relieved.

We chatter all the way down about this, that and the other. It's only about twenty minutes from Gatwick airport.

We arrive home and it's a sight for sore eyes, it really is. I don't really know what to expect. The first thing I do is get in through the front door, completely strip off, except for my boxers, and then dump all my clothes in the bin outside, and everything I owned – jumper, T-shirt, shorts, flip flops especially, they were humming – straight in the bin.

I shot straight upstairs and went into the shower. I found my shower gel and just stood in the shower crying like a girl for about ten minutes, just washing away everything. I got out of the shower, deodorant, put some aftershave on. I didn't shave, I thought I'd wait until the morning for that. I jumped on the scales and got the shock of my life 14 st 1lb. In 45 days I'd lost nearly two stone!!

I came down and sat at the table and just chatted with the guys. They'd got me a selection of cold meats and sandwiches, so I had a few bites of this, that and the other, but I couldn't really eat much because I suppose my stomach had shrunk. They'd all warned me in prison that you can't eat too much to start off with because you'll end up with massive cramps, so I just had a few bites. Finally, everybody went to bed. The kids obviously had school in the morning. Heids had work in the morning too. Heids and I went up to bed and we just laid there and chatted for hours and hours about all sorts of things, everything. Finally, we must have drifted off. It was fantastic to be home and that this whole ordeal was now finally over.

Acknowledgements

Thank you to my fantastic wife Heidi, whose efforts in securing my release were unwavering. I can't imagine what you must have gone through, just getting on that plane in Bodrum and leaving me behind must have been terrifying. You made countless phone calls and sent hundreds of emails to some very important people. You vetted many different lawyers until finally finding Murat. For what you went through I truly sorry but will always be eternally grateful.

Thank you to my family who provided support for Heidi and the boys in my absence, in particular, Zoe, Zach and Victoria. Thanks to Guy for your valuable advice, morning, noon and night. Thanks to Mumsie, Dad and Maggie for their generous input. Thanks to Amanda, Steve, Izzy and Joseph for the countless support, dinners and sleep-overs. Thanks to the Noo Na's, Nicky, James, Billy, Elle and Lou for their tireless support, dinners and Noo Na hugs. Alex, Andy, Tom and Jessica down under x. In times like these, my small but extremely strong family all pulled together and shared the load.

A huge thanks to Billy for watching my back in prison, without you my time inside would have been a whole lot worse. Thanks to Charlene, Billy's wife for getting the Birthday card out and for the countless phone calls to Heidi x.

Thank you to London Legal International and in particular Burcu Orhan Holmgren who was Heidi's primary contact in the UK. Her support was fantastic, always updating progress with the personal touch. Thank you to my friend Murat Yilmaz who runs the Turkish office in Izmir. If ever you're in trouble in Turkey then this is your man. He's approachable, knowledgeable, honest and completely tireless in his pursuit for justice.

Thank you to Tim Loughton MP, our local Conservative MP for Hove. Tim came around to the house and listened but more importantly acted immediately. He got the British government and the Foreign Office on the case, both acting faultlessly on my behalf. I know my name came up in cabinet meetings and for that I'm eternally grateful.

Thank you to the British Embassy in Turkey for your countless telephone calls to the Judge presiding over my case and for the personal touch you afforded Heidi.

Thank you to the charity, Prisoners Abroad, who provided great advise and support to my family.

Thank you to my work for your understanding during my absence, in particular, Carl for your weekly telephone calls with Heidi.

Thank you to Heidi's work, Portslade Health Centre for their support and understanding they gave. X

Thank you to the congregation of Southwick Christian Community Church in particular Pastor Lynda. X

Thank you to Jimbo for being such great help with the press. X

A great big thank you to Amanda at Bright VA. You were absolutely amazing, listening to me waffle on for six hours or so and then transcribing it all was no easy task. X

Thank you to the British press for getting behind me and my story; I never expected to make the front page!!

Thanks to my crew mates on the ambulance for listening to me waffling on for eight or ten hours at a time, whilst on shift. You know who you are. X

Finally, thank you to the great British public for your undying support and kind messages. British people hate to see injustice and this was never more prevalent during my ''extended holiday''. Thank you for caring!!

Notes

I've struggled to come to terms with just how this could happen to a bloke like me but writing this narrative has helped me immensely. However just knowing that the powers that be here in the UK were behind me has meant so much to me and my family.

* * *

I have never been so proud to be British, holding a British passport really does mean something and if you are lucky enough to hold one, don't take it for granted, treasure it forever!

* * *

Absolution:

Noun

Formal release from guilt, obligation or punishment.

''absolution from the sentence''

Synonyms: forgiveness, pardoning,
> Exoneration, remission,
> Dispensation, indulgence,
> Purgation, clemency, mercy.

* * *

Printed in Great Britain
by Amazon

63449893R00080